SAMPLERS AND
TAPESTRY EMBROIDERIES

PLATE I.—TAPESTRY EMBROIDERY. HENRY VIII., EDWARD VI., MARY, AND ELIZABETH.

The Corporation of Maidstone.

SAMPLERS & TAPESTRY EMBROIDERIES

EMBROIDERIES

BY

MARCUS B. HUISH

SECOND EDITION

DOVER PUBLICATIONS, INC.
NEW YORK

Published in Canada by General Publishing Company, Ltd., 30 Lesmill Road, Don Mills, Toronto, Ontario.

Published in the United Kingdom by Constable and Company, Ltd., 10 Orange Street, London WC 2.

This Dover edition, first published in 1970, is an unabridged and corrected republication of the second revised edition (1913; originally published by Longmans, Green, and Co., London) of the work first published in 1900 by Longmans in association with the Fine Art Society, London.

In the present edition eight of the twenty-four 1913 color plates are reproduced in color, the remainder in black and white.

Standard Book Number: 486-22070-2
Library of Congress Catalog Card Number: 78-107667

Manufactured in the United States of America
Dover Publications, Inc.
180 Varick Street
New York, N.Y. 10014

Preface to the Second Edition

I HAVE explained, in the chapter upon English Needlework with which this volume opens, the reasons which prompted me to take up the subject of Samplers and Tapestry Embroideries, and I have here only to thank the many who, since its first issue, have expressed their acknowledgment of the pleasure they have derived from it, and to record my gratification that it has induced some of them to start the study and collection of these interesting objects.

In the present edition several American Samplers of considerable interest, kindly furnished by correspondents in that country, are noted and illustrated.

I am indebted to the publishers for putting the present volume on the market at a more popular price than the expense of the first edition permitted.

PLATE I. (FRONTISPIECE.)

THE very unusual piece of Embroidery reproduced as our Frontispiece may date from the Accession of Queen Elizabeth, in which case it is the earliest specimen of an embroidery picture that we have seen. It would appear to be the creation of some exultant Protestant rejoicing at the restoration of his religion, which to him is "Good tidings of great joy"; for his Queen holds the Bible open at this verse, and is ready to defend it with her sword. Edward VI. also upholds the Bible in his upraised hand, whilst Henry VIII. has one foot on the downtrodden Pope, and the other on his crown, which he has kicked from his head. Popery is portrayed in Mary with her Rosary and Papal-crowned Dragon. The presence of the Thistle raises a doubt as to its being of the Elizabethan age, but although this flower consorts with the Rose it also does so with a pansy, which deprives it of its value as an emblem of Scotland. The piece belongs to the Corporation of Maidstone.

Tho our Countrie everywhere is fil'd

With ladies and with gentlewomen skil'd

In this rare art, yet here they may discerne

Some things to teach them if they list to learne

And as this booke some cunning workes doth teach

Too high for meane capacities to reache

So for weake learners other workes here be

As plaine and easie as an A B C.

—THE NEEDLE'S EXCELLENCY.

Contents

List of Plates

Illustrations in Text

Description of Colour Plates

The description of Plate I (frontispiece) will be found on page vi.
The eight colour plates follow page 40, and are described on pages
xiii through xv.

PLATE VI.

THIS Sampler, of which only the upper half is reproduced, is remarkable not only for the decorative qualities of its design but for its perfect state of preservation. It consists, besides the four rows which are seen, of one other in which the drawn work is subservient in quantity to the embroidery, and of seven rows in which the reverse is the case. The inscription, which is set out below, alternates in rows with those of the design. The butter colour of the linen ground is well reproduced in the plate. The original measures 32 × 8.

INSCRIPTION.

"Look Well to that thou takest in
Hand Its Better Worth Then house
Or Land   When Land is gone and
Money is spent Then learn
ing is most Excelent
Let vertue Be Thy guide and it will kee
p the out of pride Elizabeth Creasey
Her work Done in the year 1686."

PLATE VII.

THIS is a much smaller specimen than we are wont to find in "long" Samplers, for it measures only 18 × 7¼. It differs also from its fellows in that the petals of the roses in the second and third of the important bands are in relief and superimposed. The rest of the decoration, on the other hand, partakes much more of an outline character than is usual. As a specimen of a seventeenth-century Sampler it leaves little to be desired. It is signed Hannah Dawe.

PLATE X.

THE Sampler is noteworthy not only on account of its harmonious colour scheme, its symmetry of parts, and the excellence of its needlework, but as having been wrought by a young lady who afterwards became Mrs Ruskin, and the grandmother of John Ruskin. Her name, Catherine Tweedall, is worked in the lower circle, and is illegible in the otherwise admirable reproduction, owing to its being in a faded shade of the fairest pink. The verse was probably often read by her renowned grandson, and may perchance have spurred his determination to strive in the race in which he won so "high a reward." Mrs Arthur Severn, to whom the Sampler belongs, notes that the Jean Ross whose name also appears upon it was the sister of the great Arctic explorer. The date of the Sampler is 1775.

PLATE XII.

THIS "Goldfinch" Sampler was one of the most elaborate Samplers in the Bond Street Exhibition, and is really a wonderful production for a child of seven years of age. It was probably made early in the nineteenth century.

PLATE XVII.

REPRODUCES the gay and well-preserved top of a writing box. The figures which stand under a festooned bower may represent Paris handing the apple to Venus. The dress of the female is of the time of Charles I., which is the date of the casket, the interior of which is lined in part with that beautiful shade of red so popular at this time, and in part with mirrors which reflect a Flemish engraving which lines the bottom. An upper tray is a mass of ill-concealed secret drawers. Size, 12 × 11 inches.

PLATE XXI.

THE bright colouring of this picture is due to the greater portion of it having been worked in beads, in which those of strong blue and green predominate, only the hair and hands being worked in needlework, the former in knotted stitches. Beadwork seems to have been extensively utilised in seventeenth-century pictures, but it does not figure in Samplers until a late date, and then only to a minor extent. It is illustrated in Fig. 53, and is about a century old, having been included in the Fine Art Society's Exhibition.

The central figures in this piece represent Charles II. and his Queen, Catherine of Braganza, who is represented with that curious lock of hair on her forehead to which the King took so much objection when he saw it for the first time upon her arrival at Southampton. The portraits within the four circles have not at present been recognised. The late owner of this piece purchased it in Hammersmith, and from the fact that Queen Catherine had a house there it is possible that it may have once been a royal possession. Size, $13\frac{1}{2} \times 17\frac{1}{2}$.

PLATE XXII.

IN no Embroidery in the whole of this volume has a more determined endeavour been made to imitate Tapestry than in the little piece here illustrated. So deftly has this been carried out that experts have declined to believe that it is needlework, or that the gradation of blues in the background have been obtained except through stain or dye. The workmanship of that portion of the sky over which the bird flies appeared also too fine for manual execution. An examination of the back has disproved both suppositions. The piece is noteworthy for the border at the top, which is a link connecting it with the Sampler. A date, 1735, can be distinguished through the stain in the upper right corner.

PLATE XXIII.

A SPECIMEN of stitchery of various kinds, much of it in high relief, and of purl work. The reproduction, whilst translating very faithfully the colours, gives but little idea of the relief. Size, $12 \times 16\frac{1}{2}$.

PLATE II.—SAMPLER BY M. C.   16TH–17TH CENTURY.

This early pattern Sampler is described at p. 16.

FIG. 1.—THE VISIT TO THE BOARDING SCHOOL. BY GEORGE MORLAND.

Wallace Collection.

FIG. 2.—BOTTOM OF SAMPLER, IN KNOTTED YELLOW SILK, BY MARY CANEY, 1710.
Mrs C. J. Longman.

English Needlework

A MONGST all the Minor Arts practised by our ancestresses, there was certainly no one which was so much the fashion, or in which a higher grade of proficiency was attained, as that of needlework. It was in vogue in the castle and the cottage, in the ladies' seminary and the dame's school, and a girl's education began and ended with endeavours to attain perfection in it. Amongst the earliest objects to be shown to a mother visiting her daughter at school was, as is seen in the charming picture by Morland in the Wallace Collection (Fig. 1), the sampler which the young pupil had worked.[1] These early tasks were, very

[1] The picture also shows that the principal decorations of the walls of the schoolroom were framed examples of attainments with the needle.

certainly in the majority of instances, little cared for by the school-girls who produced them, but being cherished by fond parents they came in after years to be looked upon with an affectionate eye by those who had made them, and to be preserved and even handed down as heirlooms in the family.

For some reason, not readily apparent, no authority on needle-work has considered this by-product of the Art to be worthy of notice. In the many volumes which have been penned the writers have almost exclusively confined their attention to the more ambitious and, perhaps, more artistic performances of foreign nations. To such an extent has this omission extended that in a leading treatise on "Needlework as Art," samplers are dismissed in a single line, and in a more recent volume they are not even mentioned. It follows that the illustrations for such books are almost without exception culled from foreign sources, to the entire exclusion of British specimens.

It may be contended that the phase of needlework to which special attention is drawn in this volume cannot be classed amongst even the Minor Arts, and therefore is not worthy of the notoriety which such a work as this gives to it. Such a contention can fortunately be met by the authority of one whose word can hardly be challenged on such a question, namely, Mr Ruskin. Some years ago, upon a controversy arising in the press as to what objects should, and what should not, find a place in a museum, the author, in his capacity of editor of *The Art Journal*, induced Mr Ruskin to furnish that magazine with a series of letters containing his views on the matter. In these, after dealing with the planning of the building and its fitting up with the specialties which the industry of each particular district called for, he set aside six chambers for the due exposition of the six queenly and Muse-taught Arts of *Needle-work*, Writing, Pottery, Sculpture, Architecture, and Painting, and in these the absolute best in each Art, so far as attainable by the municipal pocket, was to be exhibited, the rise and fall (if fallen) of each Art being duly and properly set forth.

Mr Ruskin did not, however, content himself with claiming for needlework a prominent position. Had he only done this, his dictum might have availed us but little as regards admission of the branch of it to which we shall devote most of this volume. With the thoroughness which was so characteristic of him, he gave chapter and verse for the faith that was in him, clenching it with one of his usual felicitous instances, which, in this case, took as its text the indifferent stitching of the gloves which he used when engaged in forestry.

Proceeding to show what the needlework chamber should contain, he designated first the structure of wool and cotton, hemp, flax, and silk, then the phases of its dyeing and spinning, and the mystery of weaving. "Finally the accomplished phase of needlework, all the acicular Art of Nations—savage and civilised—from Lapland boot, letting in no snow water, to Turkey cushion bossed with pearl; to valance of Venice gold in needlework; to the counterpanes and *Samplers* of our own lovely ancestresses."

It might appear to be by an accident that he specifically included the "Samplers of our own lovely ancestresses," but this was not so. Fine needlework was an accomplishment which was carried to an exceptional pitch of excellence by his mother, and her son was proud of her achievements, for this proficiency had descended from his grandmother, whose sampler (reproduced on Plate X.) was probably present to Mr Ruskin's mind when he penned the sentence to which we have given prominence.

Having, then, such an authority for assigning to English needle-work a foremost place in any well organised museum, it may reason-ably be claimed that our literature should contain some record of the sampler's evolution and history, and that our museums should arrange any materials they may possess in an order which will enable a would-be student, or any one interested, to gain information concerning the rise and fall (for such it has been) of the industry.

It may be said that such information is not called for, but this can hardly be asserted in face of the fact that the first edition of this work, published at the considerable price of two guineas, was quickly exhausted, and demands have for some time been made for its reissue. The publication in question was the outcome of an exhibition held at The Fine Art Society, London, in 1900, at which some three hundred and fifty samplers, covering every decade since 1640, were shown. The interest taken in the display was remarkable, the reason probably being that almost every visitor possessed some specimen of the craft, but few had any idea that his or her possession was the descendant of such an ancestry, or had any claim to recognition beyond a purely personal one. Everyone then garnered information with little trouble and with unmistakable pleasure from the surprising and unexpected array, and the many requests that the collection should not be dispersed without an endeavour being made to perpetuate the information derived from an assemblage of so many selected examples led to the compilation of the present work.

When The Fine Art Society's Exhibition was first planned the intention was to confine it to samplers, which, in themselves, formed a class sufficiently large to occupy all the space which experience showed should be allotted to them in any display with which it was not desired to weary the visitor. But it was speedily found that their evolution and *raison d'être* could not be satisfactorily nor interestingly illustrated without recourse being had to the embroidered pictures alongside of which they originated, and which they subsequently supplanted, and to other articles for the decoration or identification of which samplers came into being. Consequently the collection was enlarged so as to include three sections: first the embroidered pieces which range themselves under the heading of " Pictures in imitation of Tapestry " ; then samplers ; and lastly the miscellaneous articles, such as books, dresses, coats, waistcoats, gloves, shoes, caskets, cases, purses, etc., which were broidered by those who had learned the art from sampler making, or from the use of samplers as guides.

It would, without doubt, have added interest and variety to this volume could all these classes have been considered in it, but to include the last-named would have necessitated enlarging its bulk beyond practicable limits, and, besides, it would then have covered ground, much of which has already been very satisfactorily and completely dealt with.

The work has consequently followed the lines of the Exhibition in so far as it includes " Samplers " and " Embroideries in the manner of Tapestry," which are dealt with in successive sections, and are followed by one upon the " stitchery " employed, written by Mrs Head.

PLATE III.

OWING to its great length this Sampler is not shown in its entirety. A portion of the upper part, which consists of various unconnected designs, and figures of birds, beetles, flies, and crayfish, has been omitted. In the portion illustrated is a man with a staff followed by a stag bearing a leaf in its mouth, a unicorn and lion, and the initials " A. S.," with date 1648. The bands of ornaments which follow are in several instances those which find a place nearly two centuries later as the borders of Samplers still. The lower portion is interesting for the changes which are rung upon the oak leaf and acorn. The silks of which it is made are in three colours only— blue, pink, and a yellowish green—which are worked upon a coarsish linen. Size, $34\frac{3}{4} \times 8\frac{1}{2}$. It is in the author's collection. A somewhat similar Sampler, dated 1666, is in the Victoria and Albert Museum.

PLATE III.—PORTION OF LONG SAMPLER BY A. S.   DATED 1648.

Author's Collection.

FIG. 3.—UPPER PORTION OF SAMPLER BY PUPIL IN ORPHAN SCHOOL, CALCUTTA, 1797.

Author's Collection.

PART I

Samplers

THE sampler as a pattern, or example, from which to learn varieties of needlework, whether of design or stitches, must have existed almost as long as the Art of Embroidery, which we know dates back into as distant a past as any of the Arts. But when we set about the investigation of its evolution, we did not propose to trouble our readers with the history of an infancy which would have been invested with little interest and less Art; we did, however, hope to be able to extend our illustrated record backwards to a date which would be limited only by the ravages which time had worked upon the material of which the sampler was composed—a date which would probably take us back to an epoch when the Art displayed upon it was of an unformed but still of an interesting character.

We must at the outset admit that we have been altogether disappointed in our quest. For some two hundred and fifty years, which most will admit to be a fair stretch of time, we can easily compile a record of genuinely dated and well-preserved specimens, filling not only every decade, but almost every year. The Art displayed, whether it be in design or dexterity with the needle, improves as we proceed backwards, until, in the exact centre of the seventeenth century, we arrive at a moment when little is left to be desired. We then have before us a series of samplers wherein the design is admirable, the stitches are of great variety, and the materials of which they are composed are, in an astonishing number of instances, as fresh and well preserved as those of to-day. But at that moment, to our astonishment, the stream is arrested, and the supply fails, for no, at present, discoverable reason. This sudden arrest can in no way be explained. It would appear as if, with the downfall of the monarchy under Charles I., with which it almost exactly corresponds, a holocaust had been made of every sampler that existed. It is most exasperating, for it is as if one had studied the life of a notable character backwards through its senility, old age, and manhood, to lose all trace of its youth and infancy. Nor is there any apparent reason for this failure of the output. As we shall show later on, needlework for a century previously was in the heyday of its fashion. Every article of dress and furniture was decked out with it. As an instance, the small branch of needlework which we discuss in our second part was mainly in vogue in the first half of the seventeenth century, when we are searching in vain for specimens of samplers. Samplers, too, for generations previously are recorded in the literature of the time as common objects of household furniture. The specimens even of our earliest recorded decade cover no less than five years, 1651 (three), 1649, 1648 (three), 1644, 1643, and yet beyond the last-named date we encounter an entire blank.

This cannot be the limit of dated specimens. Earlier ones must exist, but the publicity of a very well advertised exhibition, which brought notifications of samplers by the thousand, did not produce them. Neither have the public museums, nor indefatigable collectors of many years' standing, been able to obtain them, save two of the earliest years, 1643 and 1644, which have been acquired by the Victoria and Albert Museum, and of which that of 1643 is reproduced in Fig. 7. Our study of the sampler must therefore be based upon the materials at our disposal, and from these we shall analyse it with reference to its *raison d'être*, age, decorative qualities, characteristics, and the persons by whom it was worked.

The Need of Samplers

In these days of sober personal attire, in which the adornment of our houses is almost entirely confined to the products of the loom, the absorbing interest which needlework possessed, and the almost entire possession which, in the Middle Ages, it took of the manual efforts of womankind, is apt to be lost sight of. In 1583, Stubbes, in his "Anatomy of Abuses," wrote that the men were "decked out in fineries even to their shirts, which are wrought throughout with needlework of silke, curiously stitched with open seams and many other knacks besides," and that it was impossible to tell who was a gentleman "because all persons dress indiscriminately in silks, velvets, satins, damasks, taffeties, and such like." So, too, as regards the fair sex it was the same, from the Queen, who had no less than 2,000 dresses in her wardrobe, downwards. In France, almost at the same moment (in 1586), a petition was presented to Catherine de Medicis on "The Extreme Dearness of Living," setting forth that "mills, lands, pastures, woods, and all the revenues are wasted on embroideries, insertions, trimmings, tassels, fringes, hangings, gimps, needleworks, small chain stitchings, quiltings, back stitchings, etc., new diversities of which are invented daily." Everyone worked with the needle. We read that the lady just named gathered round her her daughters, their cousins, and sometimes the exiled Marie Stuart, and passed a great portion of the time after dinner in needlework. A little later Madame de Maintenon worked at embroidery, not only in her apartments, but even when riding or driving she was "hardly fairly ensconced in her carriage than she pulled her needlework out of the bag she carried with her."

The use of embroidery was not confined to personal adornment, but was employed in the decoration of the various objects which then went to make up the furniture of a house, such as curtains, bed-hangings, tablecloths, chair coverings, cushions, caskets, books, purses, and even pictures.

The luxury of the dwelling and the household had also of late increased to an extent that called for the possession of numbers of each article, whether it were clothing, table, or bed napery. Identification by marking and numbering became necessary, and as, probably, the very limited library of the house seldom contained books of ornamental lettering and numerals, samplers were made to furnish them. The evolution of the sampler is thus easily traceable. First of all consisting of decorative patterns thrown here and there without care upon the surface of a piece of canvas (see Plate II.); then of designs placed in more orderly rows, and making in themselves a harmonious whole; then added thereto alphabets and figures for the use of those who marked the linen, and as an off-shoot imitation of tapestry pictures by the additions of figures, houses, etc. Finally it was adopted as an educational task in the schools, as a specimen of phenomenal achievement at an early age, and as a means whereby moral precept might be prominently advertised.

As we have said, the samplers which have come down to us, and the age of which is certified by their bearing a date, do not extend beyond two hundred and seventy years, but those even of that age are writ all over with evidence that the sampler was then a fully developed growth, and must have been the descendant of a long line of progenitors. That they were in vogue long before this is proved by the references to them in literature as articles the use of which was a common one. Before proceeding further it may be well to cite some of these.

The earliest record which we have met with is one by the poet Skelton (1469-1529), who speaks of "the sampler to sowe on, the laces to embroide."

The next is an inventory of Edward VI. (1552), which notes a parchment book containing—

> "*Item :* Sampler or set of patterns worked on Normandy canvas, with green and black silks."

To Shakespeare we naturally turn, and are not disappointed, for we find that in his "Midsummer Night's Dream," Act iii. scene 2, Helena addresses Hermia as follows :—

> "O, is all forgot?
> All schooldays' friendship, childhood innocence?
> We, Hermia, like two artificial gods,
> Have with our needles created both one flower,
> Both on one sampler, sitting on one cushion,
> Both working of one song, both in one key,
> As if our hands, our sides, voices, and minds
> Had been incorporate."

And in "Titus Andronicus," Act ii. scene 4, Marcus speaks of Philomel as follows :—

> " Fair Philomel, she but lost her tongue,
> And in a tedious sampler sewed her mind."

Sir Philip Sidney (1554-86), in his " Arcadia," introduces a sampler as follows :—

> "And then, O Love, why dost thou in thy beautiful sampler set such a work for my desire to take out?"

And Milton in " Comus " (1634) :—

> "And checks of sorry grain will serve to ply
> The sampler, and to tear the housewife's wool."

In " The Crown Garland of Golden Roses," 1612, is " A short and sweet sonnet made by one of the Maides of Honor upon the death of Queene Elizabeth, which she sowed upon a sampler, in red silk, to a new tune of ' Phillida Flouts Me ' " ; beginning

> "Gone is Elizabeth whom we have lov'd so dear."

In the sixteenth century samplers were deemed worthy of mention as bequests ; thus Margaret Tomson, of Freston in Holland, Lincolnshire, by her will proved at Boston, 25th May 1546, gave to " Alys Pynchbeck, my systers doughter, my sampler with semes."

In Lady Marian Cust's work on embroidery, mention is made of a sampler of the reign of Henry VIII., and a rough illustration is given of it ; we have endeavoured to trace this piece, but have been unable to find it either in the possession of Viscount Middleton or of Lord Midleton, although both of them are the owners of other remarkable specimens of needlework.

It is evident from these extracts that samplers were common objects at least as early as the sixteenth century.

.   .   .   .

The sampler in its latest fashion differed very materially both in form and design from its progenitors. Consisting originally of odds and ends of decorative designs, both for embroidery and lacework, scattered without any order over the surface of a coarse piece of canvas, its first completed form was one of considerable length and narrow breadth, the length being often as much as a yard, and the breadth not more than a quarter. The reason for this may well have been the necessity of using a breadth of material which the looms then produced, for the canvas is utilised to its full extent, and is seldom cut or hemmed at the sides. Be that as it may, the shape was not an inconvenient one, for whilst its width was sufficient to display the design, its height enabled a quantity of patterns to follow one another from top to bottom. These consisted at first of designs only, in embroidery and lace, to which were subsequently added numerals and alphabets. Later followed texts, and then verses, which, with the commencement of the eighteenth century, practically supplanted ornaments. The sampler thereupon ceased to be a text-book for the latter, and became only a chart on which are set out varieties of lettering and alphabets. Still later it was transformed into a medium for the display of the author's ability in stitching, the alphabet even disappearing, and the ornament (if such it can be called) being merely a border in which to frame a pretty verse, and a means whereby empty spaces could be filled, Art at that epoch not having learnt that an empty space could be of any value to a composition. How these changes came about, with their approximate dates, may now be considered.

The Age of a Sampler

The approximate date of any sampler, which is not more than two hundred and fifty years old, should, from the illustrations given in this volume, be capable of being arrived at without much difficulty, and it is, therefore, only those undated specimens which, from their

FIG. 4.—SAMPLER OF CUT AND EMBROIDERED
WORK. EARLY 17TH CENTURY.

The late Canon Bliss.

appearance, may be older than that period that call for consideration here. They are but few in number, and a comparison of one or two of them may be of service as indicating the kind of examination to which old specimens should be subjected.

The earliest samplers present but little of the regularity of design which marks the dated ones. They were made for use and not for ornament, a combination which was probably always aimed at in those where regularity and order marked the whole. They would resemble that illustrated in Plate II., which bears evidence that it was nothing more or less than an example, whence a variety of patterns could be worked, for in almost every instance the design is shown in both an early and complete condition. It is somewhat difficult to assign a date to it, but the employment of silver and gold wirework to a greater or lesser extent in almost every part,[1] the coarse canvas upon which it is worked, and the colours, point to its being of the Elizabethan or early Jacobean period, the linked S's in Fig. 5 perhaps denoting the Stuart period. One of the two specimens of 1648 (Plate III.) continues in its upper portion this dropping of the decoration in a haphazard way on the canvas, although the greater part of it is strictly confined to rows of regular form. At first sight Fig. 4 should for the same reason be assigned to an earlier date than 1648, for the greater, and not the lesser, portion of it is embroidered without any apparent design. But more careful consideration discloses the fact that the sampler was evidently begun at the top with thorough regularity, and it was only at a later stage that the worker probably tired, and decided to amuse herself with more variety and less formality. Nor can an earlier date be assigned

[1] In the original all the small pieces of work in the upper corner near the initials are varieties of gold thread design.

FIG. 5.—PORTION OF SAMPLER. 17TH CENTURY.

FIG. 6.—PORTION OF SAMPLER OF
CUT AND EMBROIDERED WORK.
17TH CENTURY.

The late Mrs Head.

to Fig. 5 on account of the irregularity
and incompleteness of the lines, which
have evidently been carried out no further
than to show the pattern.[1]

The forms which the lettering takes
will probably be found to be one of the
best guides to the age of the early
samplers, and on this ground Fig. 6,
with its peculiar G and its reversed P
for a Q, may be earlier than 1650, although the stags and the pear-shaped

[1] It was claimed by its late owner, Mrs Egerton
Baines, that almost every line of this sampler contains Royalist emblems.   For instance, the angel
in the upper part is supposed to be Margaret of
Scotland wearing the Yorkist badge as a part of her
chatelaine ; beside her is the Tree of Life, on either
side of which are Lancastrian S's, the whole row
being symbolical of the descent of the Stuarts from
Margaret of Scotland, daughter of Henry VII.   The
next row of ornament is also the Tree of Life,
represented by a vine springing from an acorn,
by tradition a symbolical badge of Henrietta Maria,
wife of Charles I.   The next two rows are made up
of roses, acorns, and Stuart S's, which S's again
appear in the line beneath, linked with the Tree of
Life.   We refer elsewhere (p. 6) to the figures in
the bottom row (the whole of the sampler is not
shown here), and these are supposed to be Oliver
Cromwell as a tailed devil.   The sampler is neither
signed nor dated, but it clearly belongs to the first
half of the seventeenth century.   The silks employed
are almost exclusively pink, green, and blue, and
the work is of the open character found in that
illustrated in Plate III.

Fig. 7.—Samplers in the Victoria and Albert Museum. Dated 1643, 1667, and 1696.

PLATE IV.

THIS small Sampler (it measures only 17 × 7) is a remarkable testimony to the goodness of the materials used by our ancestors, and the care that has been taken in certain instances to preserve these early documents of family history. For it is over two hundred and sixty years since Elizabeth Calthorpe's very deft fingers produced what even now appears to be a very skilled performance, and every thread of silk and of the canvas groundwork is as fresh as the day that it emerged from the dyer's hands. The design is one of the unusual pictorial and ornamental combinations, the pictorial representing the Sacrifice of Isaac in two scenes.

PLATE IV.—SAMPLER BY ELIZABETH CALTHORPE. DATED 1656.

Mrs Charles Longman.

ornament beneath them are closely allied to those in Plate III., dated 1648.

Texts and mottoes also furnish a clue to age, for they extend backwards beyond 1686 on but one known sampler, namely that of Martha Salter in the Victoria and Albert Museum, dated 1651, which has the maxim, "The feare of God is an excellent gift," although on such articles as purses and the like they are to be found much earlier, and the "Sonnet to Queen Elizabeth," to which we have referred, shows that they were in vogue in 1612.

Age may also be approximated by the ornament and by the material of which the sampler is made, which differs as time goes on. The following table has been formed from many specimens that have come under my inspection; it shows the earliest date at which various forms of ornament appear on dated samplers so far as I have been able to trace them.

Adam and Eve, figure of	1709
Alphabet	1643
Border enclosing sampler	1726
Border of flowing naturalistic flowers	1730
Boxers (and until 1758)	1648
Crown	1691
Eyelet form of lettering (? Anne Gover's, *circ.* 1610)	1672
Fleur-de-Lys (see, however, Plate III.)	1742
Flower in vase	1742
Heart	1751
House	1765
Inscription	1662
Motto or text	1651
Mustard-coloured canvas	1728
Name of maker (? Anne Gover's, *circ.* 1610)	1648
Numerals	1655
Rows of ornament (latest 1741)	1648
Stag (but only common between 1758 and 1826)	1648
The Spies to Canaan	1804
Verse (? Lora Standish, *circ.* 1635)	1696

Lettering on Samplers

It is from this, rather than from any other feature, that
we trace the evolution of the sampler.   Originally a pattern sheet
of devices and ornaments, there were added to it in time alphabets
and numerals of various kinds, which the increased luxury of the
house called for as aids to the marking of the linen and clothes.
Later on the monotony of alphabets and numerals was varied by the
addition of the maker's name, the year, an old saw or two, and
ultimately flights into moral or religious verse.

Alphabets and Numerals

Although a sampler without either alphabets or numerals
would seem to be lacking in the very essence of its being, it is
almost certain that the earliest forms did not contain either, but
(like that in Plate II.) were merely sheets of decorative designs.
For the need of pattern-books of designs would as certainly precede
that of copy-books of alphabets and numerals, as the pleasure of
embroidering designs upon garments preceded that of marking their
ownership by names, and their quantity by figures.   A sampler
would seldom, if ever, be used as a text-book for children to learn
letters or figures from, except with the needle, and the need for
lettering and figuring upon them would, therefore, as we have said,
only arise when garments or napery became sufficiently common and
numerous to need marking.   This period had clearly been reached
when our earliest dated samplers were made, for, out of dated
specimens of the seventeenth century that I have examined, two-
thirds carry the alphabet upon them, and the majority have the

numerals.   It is rare to find later samplers without them, those of
the eighteenth century containing assortments of every variety of
lettering, Scottish ones especially laying themselves out for elaborately
designed and florid alphabets.   With the advent of the nineteenth
century, however, the sampler began to lose its *raison d'être*, and
quite one-half of those then made omit either the alphabet, or
numerals, or both.

Signatures

Initials, which are followed by signatures, occur upon samplers
of the earliest date.   It is true that one or two of the undated
samplers, which probably are earlier than any of the dated ones,
carry neither, but as a rule initials, or names, are found upon all the
early specimens.   Thus the early one in Plate II. has the initials
" M. C.," and the two dated in 1648 are marked respectively "A. S."
and " Rebekah Fisher," and that of 1649, " S. I. D."   In later times
unsigned samplers are the exception.

Inscriptions

The earliest inscriptions are practically only signatures, thus:
" Mary Hall is my name and when I was thirteen years of age
I ended this in 1662 "; or, somewhat amplified: "Ann Wattel is
my name with my needle and thred I ded this sam and if it hath
en beter I wold——" (Remainder illegible.)[1]
The earliest inscriptions, other than a signature such as the

---

[1] In one by Hannah Lanting, dated 1691, the orthography is "with my nedel
I rout the same," and it adds, "and Juda Hayle is my Dame."

FIG. 8.—LONG SAMPLER,
SIGNED ANN TURNER, 1686.

The late Mr A. Tuer.

foregoing, that I have met with are Lora Standish's (Fig. 43) and Miles Fletwood's referred to under "American Samplers," dated 1654 (Fig. 44), and which has the rhyme, "In prosperity friends will be plenty but in adversity not one in twenty." The next, dated 1686, has a saw which is singularly appropriate to a piece of needlework: "Apparrell thy self with ivstice and cloth thy self with chastitie so shall thov bee happi and thy works prosper. Ann Tvrner" (Fig. 8). It is dated 1686.

In Plate VI., on a sampler of the same year, we have wording which is not infrequently met with in the cycles which follow, as, for instance, in Mrs Longman's sampler, dated 1696, and in one of 1701. It runs thus :—

> "Look well to that thou takest in Hand Its better worth then house or Land. When Land is gone and Money is spent Then learning is most Excelent Let vertue be Thy guide and it will keep the out of pride Elizabeth Creasey Her Work done in the year 1686."

Dated in 1693-94 are the set of samplers recording national events, to which reference will be made elsewhere. In the last-named year (1694) a sampler bears the verse:

> "Love thou thee Lord and he will be a tender father unto thee."

And one of 1698, "Be not wise in thy own eyes."—*Sarah Chamberlain.*

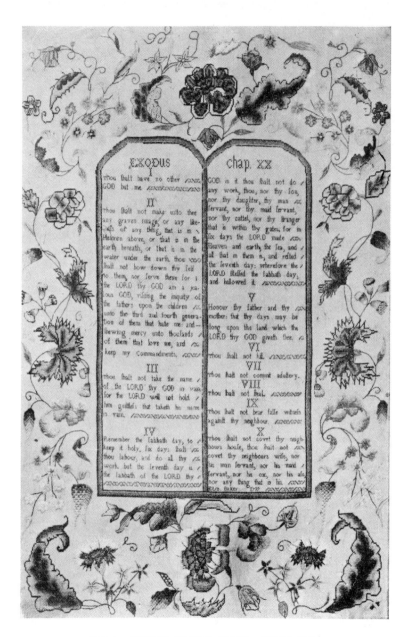

FIG. 9.—SAMPLER BY ELIZ. BAKER. DATED 1739.

PLATE V.

THIS plate only shows the upper half of a remarkably preserved Sampler. Like its fellow (*Plate VI.*) it is distinguished by its admirable decorative qualities of colour and design. The lower portion, not reproduced, consists of three rows of designs in white thread, and four rows of drawn work. The inscription, which is in the centre, and is reproduced in part, runs thus:

"MaRy HaLL IS My NaMe AnD WHen I WaS THIRTeen
     yeaRS OF AGE I ENDED THIS In 1662."

Size, 34 × 8½.

PLATE V.—PORTION OF SAMPLER BY MARY HALL. DATED 1662.

A preference for saws rather than rhymes continues until the eighteenth century is well advanced.   The following are instances :—

"If you know Christ you need know little more if not Alls lost that you have LaRnt before."—*Elizabeth Bayles*, 1703.

"The Life of Truth buteafieth Youth and maketh it lovely to behold Blessed are they that maketh it there staey and pryes it more than gold it shall be to them a ryoul diadem transending all earthly joy."
—*Elizabeth Chester*, 1712.

"Keep a strict guard over thy tongue, thine ear and thine eye, lest they betray thee to talk things vain and unlawful.   Be sparing of thy words, and talk not impertinently or in passion.   Keep the parts of thy body in a just decorum, and avoid immoderate laughter and levity of behaviour."—*Sarah Grimes*, 1730.

"Favour is deceitful And beauty is vain But a woman that feareth the Lord She shall be praised."—*Mary Gardner, aged* 9, 1740.

Another undated one of the period is :—

"Awake, arise behold thou Hast thy Life ALIFe ThY Breath ABLASt at night LY Down Prepare to have thy Sleep thy Death thy Bed Thy Grave."

One with leisure might search out the authors of the doggerel religious and moral verses which adorned samplers.   The majority are probably due to the advent of Methodism, for we only find them occurring in any numbers in the years which followed that event. It may be noted that "Divine and Moral Songs for Children," by Isaac Watts, was first published in 1720, that Wesley's Hymns appeared in 1736, and Dr Doddridge's in 1738.

We may here draw attention to the eighteenth-century fashion of setting out the Lord's Prayer and the Ten Commandments (Fig. 9), and other lengthy manuscripts from the Old Testament in tablets similar to those painted and hung in the churches of the time. The tablets in the samplers are flanked on either side by full length figures of Christ and Moses, or supported by the chubby winged cherubs of the period which are the common adornments of the Georgian gravestones. In the exhibition at The Fine Art Society's were specimens dated 1715, 1735, 1740, 1757, and 1762, the Belief taking, in three instances, the place of the Commandments. On occasions the pupil showed her proficiency in modern languages as well as with the needle, by setting out the Lord's Prayer in French, or even in Hebrew.

Contemporaneously with such lengthy tasks in lettering as the Tables of the Law, came other feats of compassing within the confines of a sampler whole chapters of the Bible, such as the 37th Chapter of Ezekiel, worked by Margaret Knowles in 1738; the 134th Psalm (a favourite one), by Elizabeth Greensmith in 1737, and of later dates the three by members of the Brontë family.

The last-named samplers (Figs. 10, 11, and 12) by three sisters of the Brontë family which, through the kindness of their owner, Mr Clement Shorter, I am able to include here, have, it will be seen, little except a personal interest attaching to them. In comparison with those which accompany them they show a strange lack of ornament, and a monotony of colour (they are worked in black silk on rough canvas) which deprive them of all attractiveness in themselves. But when it is remembered who made them, and their surroundings, these appear singularly befitting and characteristic. For, as the dates upon them show, they were produced in the interval which was passed by the sisters at home between leaving one ill-fated school, which caused the deaths of two sisters, and their passing to another. It was a mournful, straitened home in which they lived, one in which it needed the ardent Protestantism that is breathed in the texts broidered on the samplers to uphold them from a despair that can almost be

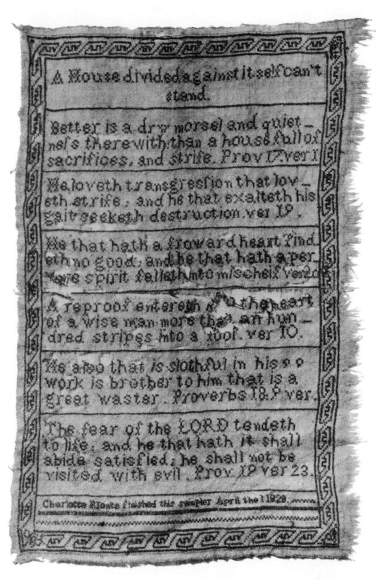

FIG. 10.—SAMPLER BY CHARLOTTE BRONTË. DATED 1829.

Mr Clement Shorter.

THE words of Agur the son of Jakeh, even the prophecy: the man spake unto Ithiel, even unto Ithiel and Ucal, Surely I am more brutish than any man, and have not the understanding of a man. I neither learned wisdom, nor have the knowledge of the holy. Who hath ascended up into heaven, or descended? who hath gathered the wind in his fists? who hath bound the waters in a garment? who hath established all the ends of the earth? what is his name, and what is his son's name, if thou canst tell? Every word of God is pure: he is a shield unto them that put their trust in him. Add thou not unto his words, lest he reprove thee, and thou be found a liar. Two things have I required of thee; deny me them not before I die: Remove far from me vanity and lies: give me neither poverty nor riches; feed me with food convenient for me: Lest I be full, and deny thee, and say, Who is the LORD? or lest I be poor, and steal, and take the name of my God in vain. 30th of Proverbs, the first 9 Verses.

The Lord is gracious, and full of compassion; slow to anger, and of great mercy. the Lord is good to all: and his tender mercies are over all his works. Psalm. CXLV. Verses 8th, 9th.

Emily Jane Brontë Finished this Sampler. March 1st 1829

YE saints on earth, ascribe, with heaven's high host,
Glory and honour to the One in Three;
To God the Father, Son, and Holy Ghost,
As was, and is, and evermore shall be.

FIG. 11.—SAMPLER BY EMILY JANE BRONTË. DATED 1829.

Mr Clement Shorter.

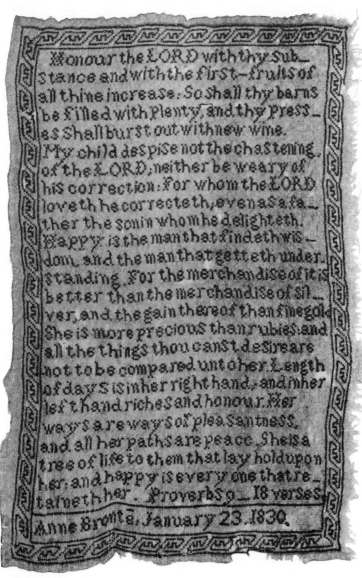

Honour the LORD with thy sub_
stance and with the first—fruits of
all thine increase. So shall thy barns
be filled with plenty, and thy press_
es shall burst out with new wine.
My child despise not the chastening
of the LORD, neither be weary of
his correction: For whom the LORD
loveth he correcteth, even as a fa_
ther the son in whom he delighteth.
Happy is the man that findeth wis_
dom, and the man that getteth under_
standing. For the merchandise of it is
better than the merchandise of sil_
ver, and the gain thereof than fine gold
She is more precious than rubies: and
all the things thou canst desire are
not to be compared unto her. Length
of days is in her right hand, and in her
left hand riches and honour. Her
ways are ways of pleasantness,
and all her paths are peace. She is a
tree of life to them that lay hold upon
her; and happy is every one that re_
taineth her. Proverbs 9 _ 18 verses.
Anne Brontë. January 23. 1830.

FIG. 12.—SAMPLER BY ANNE BRONTË. DATED 1830.

Mr Clement Shorter.

PLATE VIII.

AN early specimen of a bordered Sampler, dated 1747, the rows being relegated to a small space in the centre, where they are altogether an insignificant feature in comparison with the border. Some of the ornament to which we have been accustomed in the rows survives, as for instance the pinks, but a new one is introduced, namely, the strawberry. Here are also the Noah's Ark animals, trees, etc., which henceforward become common objects and soon transform the face of the Sampler. The border itself is in evident imitation of the worsted flower work with which curtains, quilts, and other articles were freely adorned in the early eighteenth century.

PLATE VIII.—SAMPLER BY MARY POSTLE. DATED 1747.

Mrs Head.

read between the lines. It was also, for one at least of them, a time of ceaseless activity of mind and body, and we can well understand that the child Charlotte, who penned, between the April in which her sampler was completed and the following August, the manuscript of twenty-two volumes, each sixty closely written pages, of a catalogue, did not take long to work the sampler which bears her name. The ages of the three girls when they completed these samplers were : Charlotte, 13 ; Emily Jane, 11 ; and Anne, 10.

But the lengthiest task of all was set to six poor little mortals in the Orphans' School, near Calcutta, in Bengal, East Indies. These wrought six samplers "by the direction of Mistress Parker," dividing between them the longest chapter in the Bible, namely, the 119th Psalm. It was evidently a race against time, for on each is recorded the date of its commencement and finish, being accomplished by them between the 14th of February and the 23rd of June 1797. At the top of each is a view of a different portion of the school; one of these is reproduced in Fig. 3.

Returning to the chronological aspect of sampler inscriptions. As the eighteenth century advances we find verses coming more and more into fashion, although at first they are hardly distinguishable from prose, as, for instance, in the following of 1718 :—

"You ask me why I love, go ask the glorius son, why it throw the world doth run, ask time and fat [fate ?] the reason why it flow, ask dammask rosees why so full they blow, and all things elce suckets fesh which forceeth me to love. By this you see what car my parents toock of me. Elizabeth Matrom is my name, and with my nedell I rought the same, and if my judgment had beene better, I would have mended every letter. And she that is wise, her time will pris (e), she that will eat her breakfast in her bed, and spend all the morning in dressing of her head, and sat at deaner like a maiden bride, God in His mercy may do much to save her, but what a cas is he in that must have her. Elizabeth Matrom. The sun sets, the shadows fleys, the good consume, and the man he deis."

More than one proposal has been made, in all seriousness, during the compilation of this volume, that it would add enormously to its interest and value if every inscription that could be found upon samplers were herein set out at length. It is needless to say that it has been altogether impossible to entertain such a task. It is true that the feature of samplers which, perhaps, interests and amuses persons most is the quaint and incongruous legends that so many of them bear, but I shall, I believe, have quite sufficiently illustrated this aspect of the subject if I divide it into various groups, and give a few appropriate examples of each. These may be classified under various headings.

Verses commemorating Religious Festivals

These are, perhaps, more frequent than any others. Especially is this the case with those referring to Easter, which is again and again the subject of one or other of the following verses :—

> " The holy feast of Easter was injoined
> To bring Christ's Resurrection to our Mind,
> Rise then from Sin as he did from the Grave,
> That by his Merits he your Souls may save.

> " White robes were worn in ancient Times they say,
> And gave Denomination to this Day
> But inward Purity is required most
> To make fit Temples for the Holy Ghost."

Mary Wilmot, 1761.

Or the following :—

> " See how the lilies flourish wite and faire,
> See how the ravens fed from heaven are ;

Never distrust thy God for cloth and bread
While lilies flourish and the Raven's fed."

Mary Heaviside, 1735.

Or the variation set out on Fig. 19.

As also in that by Kitty Harison, in our illustration, Fig. 13.

FIG. 13.—EASTER SAMPLER BY KITTY HARISON.   DATED 1770.

The Christmas verse is usually :—

"Glory to God in the Highest";

but an unusual one is that in Margaret Fiddes's sampler, 1773 :—

"The Night soon past, it ran so fast. The Day
Came on Amain. Our Sorrows Ceast Our Hopes
Encreast once more to Meet again A Star ap-
pears Expells all Fears Angels give Kings to
Know A Babe was sent With that intent to
Conquer Death below."

Ascension Day is marked by :—

"The heavens do now retain our Lord
Until he come again,
And for the safety of our souls
He there doth still remain.
And quickly shall our King appear
And take us by the hand
And lead us fully to enjoy
The promised Holy Land."

Sarah Smith, 1794.

Whilst Passion Week is recognisable in :—

"Behold the patient Lamb, before his shearer stands," etc.

The Crucifixion itself, although it is portrayed frequently in German samplers (examples in The Fine Art Society's Exhibition were dated 1674, 1724, and 1776), is seldom, if ever, found in English ones, but for Good Friday we have the lines :—

"Alas and did my Saviour bleed
For such a worm as I?"

Verses taking the Form of Prayers, Dedications, Etc.

Amongst all the verses that adorn samplers there were none which apparently commended themselves so much as those that dedicated the work to Christ. The lines usually employed are so familiar as hardly to need setting out, but they have frequent varieties. The most usual is :—

> "Jesus permit thy gracious name to stand
> As the first Effort of young Phoebe's hand
> And while her fingers on this canvas move
> Engage her tender Heart to seek thy Love
> With thy dear Children let her Share a Part
> And write thy name thyself upon her Heart."

Harriot Phoebe Burch, aged 7 years, 1822.

A variation of this appears in the much earlier piece of Lora Standish (Fig. 43).

Another, less common, but which again links the sampler with a religious aspiration, runs :—

> "Better by Far for Me
> Than all the Simpsters Art
> That God's commandments be
> Embroider'd on my Heart."

Mary Cole, 1759.

Verses to be used upon rising in the morning or at bedtime are not unfrequent; the following is the modest prayer of Jane Grace Marks (1807).

"If I am right, oh teach my heart
Still in the right to stay,
If I am wrong, thy grace impart
To find that better way."

But one in my possession loses, by its ludicrousness, all the impressiveness which was intended :—

"Oh may thy powerful word
Inspire a breathing worm
To rush into thy kingdom Lord
To take it as by storm.

Oh may we all improve
Thy grace already given
To seize the crown of love
And scale the mount of heaven."

Sarah Beckett, 1798.

Lastly, a prayer for the teacher :—

"Oh smile on those whose liberal care
Provides for our instruction here ;
And let our conduct ever prove
We're grateful for their generous love."

Emma Day, 1837.

Plate VI.—Portion of Sampler by Elizabeth Creasey. Dated 1686.

(*Description on page xiii*)

PLATE VII.—SAMPLER BY HANNAH DAWE. 17TH CENTURY.
(*Description on page xiii*)

She who from Heaven expects to Gain her end
Must by her own efforts her self befriend
The wretch who neer exceeds a faint desire
Goes not half way to what she would acquire
She that to virtues high rewards would rise
Must run ye race before she win ye prize

James Tweedall . Janet Adair
Jean   Rofs

Christian Anderson

PLATE X.—SAMPLER BY CATHERINE TWEEDALL.   DATED 1775.

(*Description on page xiv*)

ALL Youth, set right at first, with Ease go on,
And each new Task is with new Pleasure done,
But if neglected till they grow in Years,
And each fond Mother, her dear Darling spares,
Error becomes habitual, and you'll find,
'Tis then hard Labour to reform the Mind.

Ann Maria. Wiggins
aged seven years.

PLATE XII.—SAMPLER BY ANN MARIA WIGGINS. 19TH CENTURY.
(*Description on page xiv*)

PLATE XVII.—LID OF A CASKET. THE JUDGMENT OF PARIS. ABOUT 1630.
(*Description on page xiv*)

PLATE XXI.—BEADWORK EMBROIDERY. CHARLES II. AND HIS QUEEN, ETC.

(*Description on page xv*)

PLATE XXII.—TAPESTRY EMBROIDERY. DATED 1735.
(*Description on page xv*)

PLATE XXIII.—SPECIMEN OF PURL EMBROIDERY. 16TH–17TH CENTURY.

(Description on page xv)

Verses Referring to Life and Death

The fact that "Religion never was designed to make our pleasures less" appears seldom or never to have entered into the minds of those who set the verses for young sampler workers. From the earliest days when they plied their needle their thoughts were directed to the shortness of life and the length of eternity, and many a healthy and sweet disposition must have run much chance of being soured by the morbid view which it was forced to take of the pleasures of life. For instance, a child of seven had the task of broidering the following lines :—

> "And now my soul another year
> Of thy short life is past
> I cannot long continue here
> And this may be my last."

And one, no older, is made to declare that :—

> "Thus sinners trifle, young and old,
> Until their dying day,
> Then would they give a world of gold
> To have an hour to pray."

Or :—

> "Our father ate forbidden Fruit,
> And from his glory fell ;
> And we his children thus were brought
> To death, and near to hell."

Or again :—

> "There's not a sin that we commit
> Nor wicked word we say
> But in thy dreadful book is writ
> Against the judgment day."

A child was not even allowed to wish for length of days. Poor little Elizabeth Raymond, who finished her sampler in 1789, in her eighth year, had to ask :—

> " Lord give me wisdom to direct my ways
> I beg not riches nor yet length of days
> My life is a flower, the time it hath to last
> Is mixed with frost and shook with every blast."

A similar idea runs through the following :—

> " Gay dainty flowers go simply to decay,
> Poor wretched life's short portion flies away ;
> We eat, we drink, we sleep, but lo anon
> Old age steals on us never thought upon."

Not less lugubrious is Esther Tabor's sampler, who, in 1771, amidst charming surroundings of pots of roses and carnations, intersperses the lines :—

> " Our days, alas, our mortal days
> Are short and wretched too
> Evil and few the patriarch says
> And well the patriarch knew."

A very common verse, breathing the same strain, is :—

> " Fragrant the rose, but it fades in time
> The violet sweet, but quickly past the Prime
> White lilies hang their head and soon decay
> And whiter snow in minutes melts away
> Such and so with'ring are our early joys
> Which time or sickness speedily destroys."

And the melancholy which pervades the verse on the sampler of Elizabeth Stockwell (Fig. 14) is hardly atoned for by the brilliant hues in which the house is portrayed.

FIG. 14.—SAMPLER BY ELIZABETH STOCKWELL. 1832.

The late Mr A. Tuer.

The gruesomeness of the grave is forcibly brought to notice in a sampler dated 1736 :—

> " When this you see, remember me,
> And keep me in your mind ;
> And be not like the weathercock
> That turn att every wind.
> When I am dead, and laid in grave,
> And all my bones are rotten,
> By this may I remembered be
> When I should be forgotten."

Ann French put the same sentiment more tersely in the lines :—

> " This handy work my friends may have
> When I am dead and laid in grav." 1766.

It is a relief to turn to the quainter and more genuine style of Marg't Burnell's verse taken from Quarles's " Emblems," and dated 1720 :—

> " Our life is nothing but a winters day,
> Some only breake their fast, & so away,
> Others stay dinner, & depart full fed,
> The deeper age but sups and goes to bed.
> Hee's most in debt, that lingers out the day,
> Who dyes betimes, has lesse and lesse to pay."

This verse has crossed the Atlantic, and figures on American samplers.

But the height of despair was not reached until the early years of the nineteenth century, when " Odes to Passing Bells," and such like, brought death and the grave into constant view before the young and hardened sinner thus :—

ODE TO A PASSING BELL

" Hark my gay friend that solemn toll
Speaks the departure of a soul
'Tis gone, that's all we know not where,
Or how the embody'd soul may fare
Only this frail & fleeting breath
Preserves me from the jaws of death
Soon as it fails at once I'm gone
And plung'd into a world not known."

Ann Gould Seller, Hawkchurch, 1821.

Samplers oftentimes fulfilled the rôle of funeral cards, as, for instance, this worked in black :—

" In memory of my beloved Father
John Twaites who died April 11 1829.
Life how short—Eternity how long.
Also of James Twaites
My grandfather who died Dec. 31, 1814.

How loved, how valu'd once, avails thee not
To whom related, or by whom begot,
A heap of dust alone remains of thee,
'Tis all thou art, and all the proud shall be."

Curiously enough, whilst compiling this chapter the writer came across an artillery non-commissioned officer in the Okehampton Camp who, in the intervals of attending to the telephone, worked upon an elaborate Berlin woolwork sampler, ornamented with urns, and dedicated "To the Memory of my dear father," etc.

Duties to Parents and Preceptors

That the young person who wrought the sampler had very
much choice in the selection of the saws and rhymes which inculcate
obedience to parents and teachers is hardly probable, and it is not
difficult to picture the households or schools where such doctrines
as the following were set out for infant hands to copy :—

> "All youth set right at first, with Ease go on,
>   And each new Task is with new Pleasure done,
>   But if neglected till they grow in years
>   And each fond Mother her dear Darling spares,
>   Error becomes habitual and you'll find
>   'Tis then hard labour to reform the Mind."

The foregoing is taken from the otherwise delightful sampler
worked by a child with the euphonious name of Ann Maria Wiggins,
in her seventh year, that is reproduced in Plate XII.

Preceptors also appear to have thought it well to early impress
upon pliable minds the dangers which beset a child inclined to
thoughts of love :—

> "Oh Mighty God that knows how inclinations lead
>   Keep mine from straying lest my Heart should bleed.
>
> Grant that I honour and succour my parents dear
>   Lest I should offend him who can be most severe.
>
> I implore ore me you'd have a watchful eye
>   That I may share with you those blessings on high.
>
> And if I should by a young youth be Tempted.
>   Grant I his schemes defy and all He has invented."
>
> *Elizabeth Bock*, 1764.

Samplers were so seldom worked by grown-up folk that one can hardly believe that the following verse records an actual catastrophe to the peace of mind of Eleanor Knot :—

ON DISINGENUITY

> "With soothing wiles he won my easy heart
> He sigh'd and vow'd, but oh he feigned the smart;
> Sure of all friends the blackest we can find
> Are those ingrates who stab our peace of mind."

A not uncommon and much more agreeable verse sets forth the duties of man towards woman in so far as matrimony is concerned :—

> "Adam alone in Paradise did grieve
> And thought Eden a desert without Eve,
> Until God pitying his lonesome state
> Crown'd all his wishes with a lovely mate.
> Then why should men think mean, or slight her,
> That could not live in Paradise without her."

Samplers bearing the foregoing verse are usually decorated with a picture of our first parents and the Tree of Knowledge, supported by a demon and angel.

The parent or teacher sometimes spoke through the sampler, as thus, in Lucia York's, dated 1725 :—

> "Oh child most dear
> Incline thy ear
> And hearken to God's voice."

Or again :—

> "Return the kindness that you do receive
> As far as your ability gives leave."

Mary Lounds.

"Humility I'd recommend
Good nature, too, with ease,
Be generous, good, and kind to all,
You'll never fail to please."

Susanna Hayes.

Samplers Expatiating upon Virtue or Vice, Wealth or Poverty, Happiness or Misery

Amongst these may be noted :—

"Happy is he, the only man,
Who out of choice does all he can
Who business loves and others better makes
By prudent industry and pains he takes.
God's blessing here he'll have and man's esteem,
And when he dies his works will follow him."

Of those dealing with wealth or poverty none, perhaps, is more incisive than this :—

"The world's a city full of crooked streets,
And Death's the market-place where all men meet ;
If life was merchandise that men could buy
The rich would always live, the poor alone would die."

An American sampler has the following from Burns's "Grace before Meat" :—

"Some men have meat who cannot eat
And some have none who need it.
But we have meat and we can eat,
And so the Lord be thanked."

Inscriptions having an Interest owing to their Quaintness

The following dates from 1740, and has as appendix the line, "God prosper the war" :—

> "The sick man fasts because he cannot eat
> The poor man fasts because he hath no meat
> The miser fasts to increase his store
> The glutton fasts because he can eat no more
> The hypocrite fasts because he'd be condemned
> The just man fasts cause he hath offended."

An American version of this ends with :—

> "Praise God from whom all blessings flow
> We have meat enow."

That self-conceit was not always considered a failing, is evident from the following verses :—

> "This needlework of mine may tell
> That when a child I learned well
> And by my elders I was taught
> Not to spend my time for nought,"

which is concentrated and intensified in one of Frances Johnson, worked in 1797 :—

> "In reading this if any faults you see
> Mend them yourself and find no fault in me."

In a much humbler strain is this from an old sampler in Mrs Longman's collection :—

"When I was young I little thought
That wit must be so dearly bought
But now experience tells me how
If I must thrive, then I must bowe
And bend unto another will,
That I might learn both arte & skill."

Owing to the portrayal of an insect, which was not infrequently met with in days gone by, upon the face of the sampler which bears the following lines, it has been suggested that they were presumably written by that creature :—

"Dear Debby
I love you sincerely
My heart retains a grateful sense of your past kindness
When will the hours of our
Separation be at an end?
Preserve in your bosom the remembrance
of your affectionate
Deborah Jane Berkin."

The following, coming about the date when the abolition of the slave trade was imminent, may have reference to it :—

"THERE'S mercy in each ray of light, that mortal eye e'er saw,
There's mercy in each breath of air, that mortal lips can draw,
There's mercy both for bird, and beast, in God's indulgent plan,
There's mercy for each creeping thing—But man has none for man."

Elizabeth Jane Gates Aged 12 *years* 1829.

Riddle samplers, such as that of Ann Witty, do not often occur :—

"I had both		and a		by both I set great store
I lent my	Money	to my	Friend	and took his word therefor
I asked my		of my		and nought but words I got
I lost my		and my		for sue him, I would not."

Here, too, is an "Acrostick," the first letters of whose lines spell the name of the young lady who "ended" it "Anno Dom. 1749."

> "A virgin that's Industrious Merits Praise,
> Nature she Imitates in Various Ways,
> Now forms the Pink, now gives the Rose its blaze.
> Young Buds, she folds, in tender Leaves of green,
> Omits no shade to beautify her Scene,
> Upon the Canvas, see, the Letters rise,
> Neatly they shine with intermingled dies,
> Glide into Words, and strike us with Surprize."
>
> *E. W.*

As illustrations of tales the sampler of Sarah Young (Fig. 15) is an unusual example. It deals with Sir Richard Steele's story of the loves of Inkle and Yarico. Inkle, represented as a strapping big sailor, was cast away in the Spanish Main, where he met and loved Yarico, an Indian girl, but showed his baseness by selling her for a slave when he reached Barbadoes in a vessel which rescued him. The story evidently had a considerable, if fleeting, popularity, for it was dramatised.

The Design, Ornament and Colouring of Samplers

Whilst important clues to the age of a sampler may be gathered from its form and legend, its design and colouring are factors from which almost as much may be learnt.

Design can be more easily learned from considering in detail the illustrations, which have been mainly chosen for their typifying one or other form of it, but certain general features are so usually present that they may be summarised here.

No one with any knowledge of design can look through the specimens of samplers selected for this volume without noting, first, that it is, in the earlier specimens, appropriate to the subject, decorative in treatment, and lends itself to a variety of treatment with the needle. Secondly, that the decoration is not English in origin, but is usually derived from foreign sources. Indeed, if we are to believe an old writer of the Jacobean time, the designs were

> "Collected with much praise and industrie,
> From scorching Spaine and freezing Muscovie,
> From fertile France and pleasant Italie,
> From Poland, Sweden, Denmarke, Germanie,
> And some of these rare patterns have been set
> Beyond the boundes of faithlesse Mahomet,
> From spacious China and those Kingdomes East
> And from great Mexico, the Indies West.
> Thus are these workes farre fetch't and dearly bought,
> And consequently good for ladyes thought."

Thirdly, that after maintaining a remarkable uniformity until the end of the seventeenth century, design falls away, and with rare exceptions continuously declines until it reaches a mediocrity to which the term can hardly be applied.

The same features are noticeable in the colouring. The samplers of the Caroline period are in the main marked by a softness and delicacy, with a preference for tender and harmonious shades of pinks, greens, and blues, but these quickly pass out of the schemes of colouring until their revival a few years ago through the influence of Japan and the perspicuity of Sir Lazenby Liberty. This delicacy

FIG. 15.—SAMPLER BY SARAH YOUNG. ABOUT 1750.

Mrs Head.

PLATE IX.

WERE it not that this Sampler was produced by little Miss Philips at the tender age of seven. there would be a probability that it was unique through its containing a portrait of the producer. For in no other example have we so many evidences pointing to its being a record of actual facts. For instance, there is clearly shown a gentleman pointing to his wife (in a hooped costume), and having round him his five girls of various ages, the youngest in the care of a nurse. In the upper left corner is his son in charge of a tutor, whilst on the right are two maid-servants, one being a woman of colour. This fashion for black servants is further emphasised by the Negro boy with the dog. That these should be present in this family is not remarkable, for by the lower illustration it is evident that Mr Philips was a traveller who had crossed the seas in his ship to where alligators, black swans and other rare birds abounded. The work was executed in 1761, the second year of George the Third, whose monogram and crown are supported by two soldiers in the costume of the period. It has been most dexterously carried out by the young lady, and it is conceived in a delicate harmony of greens and blues which was not uncommon at that time. Size, 19 × 12½. An adaptation of this Sampler has been utilised as the drop scene to the play of " Peter Pan."

PLATE IX.—SAMPLER BY E. PHILIPS. DATED 1761.

Author's Collection.

is not, as some suppose, due to time having softened the colours, for examination shows that fading has seldom taken place, in fact one of the most remarkable traits of the earlier samplers is the wonderful condition of their colouring (see Mrs Longman's sampler of 1656, Plate IV., as an example). Towards the end of the seventeenth century the adoption of a groundwork of roughish close-textured canvas of a canary hue also militated against this ensemble of the colour scheme, which is now and again too vivid, especially in the reds, a fact which may, in part, be due to their retaining their original tint with a persistency that has not endured with the other dyes.

During the early Georgian era sampler workers seem to have passed through a stage of affection for deep reds, blues, and greens, with which they worked almost all their lettering. The same colours are met with in the large embroidered curtains of the time; it is probably due to the influence of the tapestries and the Chinese embroideries then so much in vogue.

In the opening years of the eighteenth century a pride in lettering gave rise to a series of samplers of little interest or artistic value, consisting, as they did, of nothing else than long sentences, not readily readable, and worked in silks in colours of every imaginable hue used indiscriminately, even in a single word, without any thought bestowed on harmony or effect of colouring.

Later on, towards the middle of the century, more sober schemes of colour set in, consisting in the abandonment of reds and the employment of little else than blues, greens, yellows, and blacks (see Plate IX.), which are attractive through their quietness and unity. Subsequently but little praise can be bestowed upon samplers so far as their design is concerned. Occasionally, as in that of Mr Ruskin's ancestress (Plate X.), a result which is satisfactory, both in colour and design, is arrived at, but this is generally due to individual taste rather than to tuition or example. In this respect samplers only follow in the wake of all the other arts—furniture and silversmiths' work, perhaps, excepted, as regards both of which the taste displayed was also individual rather than national.

An evil which cankered later sampler ornamentation was a desire for novelty and variety.   The earliest samplers exhibit few signs of attempts at invention in design.   A comparison of any number of them shows ideas repeated again and again with the slightest variation.   The same floral motives are adapted in almost every instance, and one and all may well have been employed since the days when they arrived from the Far East, brought, it may be, by the Crusaders.   But it is in no derogatory spirit that I call attention to this lack of originality.   A craftsman is doing a worthier thing in assimilating designs which have shown their fitness by centuries of use, patterns which are examples of fine decorative ornament that really beautifies the object to which it is applied, than in inventing weak and imperfect originals.   No architect is accused of plagiarism if he introduces the pointed arch, and the great designs of the past are free and out of copyright.   The Greek fret, or the Persian rose, is as much the property of anyone as the daisy or the snowdrop, and it was far better to make sound decorative pieces of embroidery on the lines of these than to attempt, as was done later on, feeble originals, which have nothing ornamental or decorative in their composition.   The workers of the East, when perfection was arrived at in a design, did not hesitate to reproduce it again and again for centuries.

But the mistress of a ladies' improving school would hardly like her pupils to copy time after time the same designs—designs which perhaps resembled those of a rival establishment.   Such a one would be oblivious to the fact that an ornamentalist is born not made, that the best design is traditional, and that pupils would be far more worthily employed in perpetuating ornamentation which had been invented by races intuitively gifted for such a purpose, than in attempting feeble products of her own brain. So, too, results show that she was, as a rule, unaware that good design is better displayed in simplicity than in pretentiousness. As that authority on design, the late Lewis Day, wrote in his volume on Embroidery, " The combination of a good designer and worker in the same person is an ideal very occasionally to be met with, and any attempt to realise it generally fails."

Samplers show in increasing numbers as the end approaches that their designers were ignorant of most of the elementary rules of ornamentation in needlework, such, for instance, as that the pictorial is not a suitable subject for reproduction, nor the delineation of the human figure, nor that the floral and vegetable kingdom, whilst lending itself better than aught else, should be treated from the decorative, and not the realistic point of view.

We will now pass on to consider generally the forms of decoration most usually met with.

Sampler Design : the Human Figure

Whilst embroideries in imitation of tapestries deal almost entirely with the portrayal of the human figure, samplers of the same period, and that the best, for the most part avoid it. This is somewhat remarkable, for the design of the Renaissance, which was universally practised at the time upon which we are dwelling, was almost entirely given up to weaving it into other forms, and the volumes which treat of embroidery show how frequently it occurs in foreign pieces of needlework. The omission is a curious one, but the reason for it is, apparently, not far to seek. If we examine the earlier pieces we shall see that practically one type of figure only presents itself. Save in exceptional pieces, such as Mrs Longman's early piece (Plate IV.), where the figures are clearly copied from one of the small tapestry pieces so in vogue at that date (1656), or Mrs Millett's piece (Fig. 16), the figures which appear upon samplers are all cast in one mould, and in no way improve but rather mar the composition.

This last-named drawn-work sampler is a specimen altogether apart for beauty of design and workmanship. Doubts have been expressed as to its English origin, but portions of the ornament, such as the acorn, and the Stuart S in the lowest row, are thoroughly English ; besides, as we have seen, design in almost every one of the seventeenth-century samplers is infected with foreign motives. The uppermost panel is supposed to represent Abraham, Sarah, and the Angel. To the left is the tent, with the folds worked in relief, in a stitch so fine as to defy ordinary eyesight. Sarah, who holds up a hand in astonishment at the angel's announcement, has her head-dress, collar, and skirt in relief, the latter being sewn with microscopic fleurs-de-lis. The winged angel to the left of Abraham has a skirt composed of tiny scallops, which may represent feathers. A rabbit browses in front of the tent. The centre of the second row is occupied by a veiled mermaid, her tail covered with scalloped scale in relief. She holds in either hand a cup and a mask. The lettering in the two flanking panels is " S.I.D. 1649 A.I." The decorative motive of the outer panels is peapods in relief, some open and disclosing peas. Roses and tulips fill the larger square below, and these are followed by a row (reversed) of tulips and acorns. Four other rows complete the sampler, which only measures $18\frac{1}{2} \times 6\frac{3}{4}$. In order to give it a larger size the lowest row is not reproduced. I have seen another drawn-work sampler which antedates that just described by a year. It is of somewhat coarse texture but is good in design, and bears in a panel at the side initials and the date. The Victoria and Albert Museum has also two somewhat similar drawn-work samplers—one by Elizabeth

FIG. 16.—DRAWN-WORK SAMPLER BY S. I. D. DATED 1649.

Mrs C. F. Millett.

PLATE XI.

INCONGRUITY between the ornament and the lettering of a Sampler could hardly be carried to a more ludicrous extreme than in Ann Chapman's, which is reproduced opposite. The two points of Agur's prayer, which fills the panel, are that before he dies vanity shall be removed far from him, and that he shall have neither poverty nor riches. Yet as surroundings and supporters to this appeal we have two figures posing as mock shepherd and shepherdess, and decked out in all the vanities of the time. Agur's prayer was apparently often selected, for we see it again in the Sampler of Emily Jane Brontë (Fig. 10), but there it has the quietest of ornament to surround it, and it is worked in black silk ; whereas in the present case there is no Sampler in the collection where the whole sheaf of colours has been more drawn upon.

PLATE XI.—SAMPLER BY ANN CHAPMAN. DATED 1779.

Mrs C. J. Longman.

Wood, dated 1666, which contains the Stuart S's; the other (undated) has the arms of James I.

A type of figure pre-valent in early samplers has puzzled collectors who pos-sess specimens containing it. It wears a close-fitting costume and has arms ex-tended, and has received the name of a "Boxer," presumably from its attitude and costume. It and a com-panion are continuously de-picted for nearly a century, finally disappearing about 1742, but maintaining their attitude with less variation than any other form of ornament, the only alteration being in the form of the trophy which they hold in one hand. It is this trophy, if we may use such a term, that negatives the idea of their being combatant figures, and it almost with certainty places them in the category of the Greek Erotes, the Roman Am-ores, or the Cupids of the Renaissance. It is difficult to give a name to the

FIG. 17.—SAMPLER BY JEAN PORTER. 1709-10.

trophy in most of the samplers, and the worker was clearly often in doubt as to its structure. In some it resembles a small vase with a lid, in others a spray with branches or leaves on either side. In one of 1673 it takes the form of a four-petalled flower, and in one of 1679 that of an acorn, which is repeated in samplers of 1684, 1693, and 1694, this repetition being probably due to the acorn being a very favourite subject for design under the Stuarts. In a sampler of 1693 acorns are held in either hand. In one of 1742 (Fig. 18), the object held is a kind of candelabra. The little figures themselves preserve a singular uniformity of costume, which again points to their being the nude Erotes, clothed, to suit the times, in a tight-fitting jerkin and drawers. These are always of gayest colours. On occasions (as in a sampler dated 1693) they don a coat, and have long wigs, bringing them into line with the prevailing fashion.

When these figures disappear their place is taken by those of our first parents in the Garden of Eden, the incongruity of which is well depicted in the sampler illustrated in Fig. 17. This piece of work, which took nearly a year to complete—it was begun on 14th May 1709, and finished on 6th April 1710—is unlike any other that I have seen of that period, for it antedates, by nearly half a century, the scenes from real life which afterwards became part and parcel of every sampler. Adam and Eve became quite common objects on samplers after 1760.[1]

Mention need only be made here of the dressed figures which occur in samplers dated during the reign of George the Third. They are sometimes quaint (as in Plates IX. and XI.), but they

---

[1] The lower portion of Fig. 18 opposite introduces us to an early and crude representation of Adam and Eve and the serpent, and to the bird and fountain, and flower in vase, forms of decoration which became at a later date so very common. The name of the maker has been obliterated owing to dirt getting through a broken glass, but the date is 1742.

FIG. 18.—SAMPLER. NAME ILLEGIBLE. DATE 1742.

Formerly in the Author's Collection.

PLATE XIII.

MR JOSEPH PENNELL'S Sampler, which finds a place here as a specimen of American work, has little to distinguish it from its fellows that were produced in England in the reign of George IV. The border, it is true, only preserves its uniformity on two of the four sides, but where it does it is designed on an old English pattern, that of the wild strawberry. So, too, we find the ubiquitous stag and coach dogs, Noahs, ash trees, birds, and flower baskets.

The sampler text reads:

When wealth to virtuous hands is given
It blesses like the dews of heaven
Like heaven it hears the orphans cries
And wipes the tears from widows eyes

Martha C Barton
work 1825

PLATE XIII.—AMERICAN SAMPLER BY MARTHA C. BARTON. DATED 1825.

Mr Joseph Pennell.

hardly come into any scheme of decoration. The squareness of the stitch used in later samplers renders any imitation of painting such as was attempted altogether a failure.

Sampler Design: Animals

Animals in any true decorative sense hardly came into sampler ornament. Whilst the tapestry pictures teem with them, so that one wanting in a lion or stag is a rarity, in samplers, probably, the difficulty of obtaining rounded forms with the stitch used in the large grained canvas was a deterrent. The lion only being found on the Fletwood sampler of 1654 (Fig. 44) and the stag, which in tapestry pictures usurps the place of the unicorn, appears but rarely on samplers before the middle of the eighteenth century, when it came into fashion, and afterwards occurs with uninterrupted regularity so long as samplers were made.

This neglect of animals is hardly to be deplored, for when they do occur they are little else than caricatures (see, for instance, those in Plate III.). Birds, which lend themselves to needlework, appear in the later samplers (Plate XI. and Fig. 18), but hardly as part of any decorative scheme.

Sampler Design: Flowers

With the practically insignificant exceptions which we have just noticed, the ornamentation of the sampler was confined to floral and geometrical motives, and whilst the latter were for the most part used in drawn-work samplers, the former constituted the stock whence the greater part of the decoration employed in the older examples was derived.

Amongst the floral and vegetable kingdom the selection was a wide one, but a few favourites came in for recognition in almost every sampler, partly because of their decorative qualities, and partly from their being national badges. With few exceptions they were those which were to be met with in English seventeenth-century gardens, and undoubtedly, in some instances, may have been adapted by the makers from living specimens. Chief among the flowers was the rose, white and red, single and double, the emblem for centuries previously of two great parties in the State, a badge of the Tudor kings, a part of the insignia of the realm, and occupying a foremost place upon its coinage. In sampler ornamentation it is seldom used either in profile or in bud, but generally full face, and more often as a single than as a double flower. As a form of decoration it may have been derived from foreign sources, but it clearly owed its popularity to the national significance that attached to it.

The decorative value of the pink or carnation has been recognised from the earliest times, and a piece of Persian ornament is hardly complete without it. It is not surprising, therefore, that the old sampler workers utilised it to the full, and in fact it appears oftener than the rose in seventeenth-century specimens. Ten of the thirteen exhibits of that century at The Fine Art Society's Exhibition in 1900 contained it as against seven where the rose was figured. It maintains this position throughout, and the most successful of the borders of bordered samplers are those where it is utilised. Specimens will be found in Plates III., IV., and VI.

The decorative value of the honeysuckle was hardly appreciated, and it only appeared on samplers of the date of 1648 (Plate III.), 1662 (Plate V.), 1668, 1701, and 1711, in the Exhibition, and the undated one reproduced in Fig. 4.

Sampler workers were very faithful to the strawberry, which, after appearing in almost every one of the seventeenth-century long samplers, was a favourite object for the later borders, and it may be

FIG. 19.—SAMPLER BY MARY ANDERSON. 1831.

Lady Sherborne.

seen almost unaltered in specimens separated in date by a century at least. We give in Fig. 31 a very usual version of it. (See also Plate XIII.)

Other fruits and flowers which now and again find a place are the fig, which will be seen in Plate III.; the pineapple, the thistle (Fig. 21), and the tulip in samplers dated 1662, 1694, 1760, and 1825 (Plate XIII.).

Although the oak tree acquired political significance after the flight of Charles II., that fact can in no way account for such prominence being attached to its fruit and its foliage as, for instance, is the case in samplers dated 1644 and 1648 (Plate III.), where varieties of these are utilised in a most decorative fashion in several of the rows of ornament, or in another of the following years (Fig. 16). But, curiously enough, after appearing in almost every seventeenth-century sampler, it disappeared entirely at the commencement of the eighteenth century.

Sampler Design : Crowns, Coronets, Etc.

The crown seems to have been suddenly seized upon by sampler makers as a form of decoration, and for half a century it was used with a tiresome reiteration. It had, of course, been largely used in Tudor decoration, and on the restoration of the monarchy it would be given prominence. But it probably was also in vogue because it lent itself to filling up spaces caused by alphabets not completing a line, and also because it allowed of variation through the coronets used by different ranks of nobility. We have seen in the sampler, Fig. 20, that the coronet of each order was used with a letter beneath, indicating duke, earl, etc. On occasions crowns were also used with some effect as a border. It is possible that the fashion for coronets was

FIG. 20.—SAMPLER. SCOTTISH (?). 18TH CENTURY.

Formerly in the Author's Collection.

NOTE.—The bright colouring, coarse canvas, and ornate lettering of this piece suggest a Scottish origin. It dates from about 1730, and is one of the earliest of the bordered samplers, the border being at present an altogether insignificant addition. It is also one of the first specimens of decoration with crowns and coronets, the initials underneath standing for king, duke, marquis, earl, viscount, lord, count, and baron.

PLATE XIV.

ONE of the quaintest of the Embroidery pictures. Differing as it does from the majority of its fellows in the costume of its figures, and valuable as it is as a record of the dress of the first years of the seventeenth century, the piquancy and variety of the subjects depicted combine with these to give it an unusual interest. As regards the dress, it denotes a period towards the close of the reign of James I. The ruff is still worn by the doctors, but the boots of the gentleman who walks with a lady are very close to the fashion of Charles I. The subjects combine religious and mundane. The former comprise Christ in the Temple instructing the doctors, Susannah and the Elders, and a remarkable scene of Martyrs at the stake, one of the latter being in the uncomfortable position of having a stone protruding from his forehead. The latter show the squire and his lady beside their residence, young ladies out for an airing, and others about to enter a Pergola. Its maker has not only been happy through the vitality imparted to the human puppets, but has succeeded equally well with animal life ; witness the rabbit and squirrel beneath the apple tree and the greyhound and hare in the lower corner. The water in which Susannah laves her legs is worked in imitation of ripples, and looks fresher than the rest owing to the recent removal of the talc with which it was covered. The clouds in the upper part and the moss, etc., in the lower portion come dark in the reproduction as they are made of purl, which has tarnished. It will be noted that those of the pictures in which the surface is not entirely covered with embroidery are usually worked upon white satin. This was a fashion of the time, and supplanted velvet, the material hitherto used, owing, it is assumed, to its being an easier material to work upon, but also probably to its beautiful surface resembling a background of parchment, and to the magnificent quality which was then made.

PLATE XIV.—EMBROIDERED PICTURE: CHRIST IN THE TEMPLE, STONING OF MARTYRS, ETC.
ABOUT 1625.

Formerly in the Author's Collection.

derived from foreign samplers, where this form of decoration was frequently used about the end of the seventeenth century, doubtless owing to the abundance of ennobled personages; they may well have come over with many other fancies which followed in the train of the House of Hanover. The earliest sampler in the Exhibition before referred to which bore a crown was one of 1693; but the coronet was there placed in conjunction with the initials M. D., and might be that of a titled lady who worked it. After that it appeared in one dated 1705 (where it was clearly a royal one connected with "Her Majesti Queen Anne"), and in samplers dated 1718, 1726, 1728 (1740, in which there were at least fifty varieties), and so on almost yearly up to 1767, after which it gradually disappeared, two only out of seventy subsequent samplers containing it. These were dated 1798 and 1804. In countries

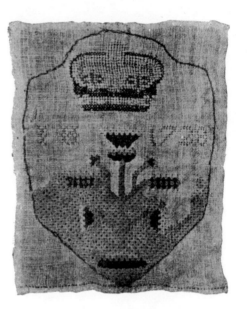

FIG. 21.—SAMPLER BY J. H. [JANE HEATH].
A.D. 1725. *Mr Ashby Sterry.*

where almost every family bore a rank which warranted the use of a coronet, there would be a reason for their appearance as part of what would have to be embroidered on table linen, etc.

The tiny sampler with crown illustrated in Fig. 21 was one of four contributed to the Exhibition by Mr Ashby Sterry, each of them representing a generation in his family. It is unfinished, the background only having been completed in the lower half; its crown and thistle denote its Scottish origin.

FIG. 22.—SAMPLER BY MARY BYWATER. 1751.

Formerly in the Author's Collection.

FIG. 23.—HEART-SHAPED SAMPLER BY MARY IVES. DATED 1796.

Miss Haldane.

NOTE.—This delightful little sampler is reproduced in its full size, and is most delicately adorned with a pink frilled ribbon edging. We do not know which of the three ladies whose names it bears worked it, or to which of them the lines, "Be unto me kind and true as I be unto you," were addressed. The date, it will be seen, is 1796, and it shows that at the end of the century there was still an affection for the little flying Cupids so usual upon eighteenth-century gravestones. We have remarked upon the absence of the cross in samplers; even here we do not find it, although we have the heart and anchor.

PLATE XV.

THE common subject amongst Tapestry workers of Hagar and Ishmael is told somewhat fully here in three scenes. In the first we have Sarah and Isaac at the tent door, in the second Abraham dismissing Hagar, and in the third the angel visiting Ishmael in the desert.

The embroidery is one of those where flat and raised work are conjoined. The sky might be woven, so fine are the stitches, the landscape is made up of a variety of open stitches which are used in lace, but in this instance have been worked on the canvas, the faces are modelled in cotton wool and covered with silk, and the animals (lion and stag) are similarly modelled. The piece is the property of Miss Taintor, of Hartford, U.S.A. Size, $14\frac{1}{2} \times 19\frac{1}{2}$.

PLATE XV.—TAPESTRY EMBROIDERY. THE STORY OF HAGAR AND ISHMAEL. ABOUT 1630.

Sampler Design : Hearts

This emblem, which one would have imagined to be a much more favourite device with impressionable little ladies than the crown, is more seldom met with. In fact, it only figured on four of the hundreds of samplers which composed the Exhibition, and in three of these cases it was in conjunction with a crown. When it is remembered how common the heart used to be as an ornament to be worn, and how it is associated with the crown in foreign religious Art, its infrequency is remarkable. The unusually designed small sampler (the reproduction being almost the size of the original), Fig. 22, dated 1751, simply worked in pale blue silk, on a fine khaki-coloured ground, has a device of crowns within a large heart. Fig. 23 shows a sampler in the form of a heart, and has, in conjunction with this symbol, anchors. It is dated 1796.

The Borders to Samplers

The sampler with a border was the direct and natural outcome of the sampler in "rows." A case, for instance, probably occurred, as in Fig. 24,[1] where a piece of decoration had a vacant space at its sides, and resort was at once had to a portion of a row, in this case actually the top one. From this it would follow

---

[1] This sampler is interesting owing to its drawn-work figures, which are directly copied from two effigies of the reign of James I., and may stand for that Monarch and his Queen. This portion of the sampler might readily be mistaken for that date were it not that it bears on the bar which divides the figures the letters S.W., 1700. The border at the side of the figures is in red silk, that at the top and the alphabet are in the motley array of colours to which we are accustomed in specimens of this date.

as a matter of course that the advantage, from a decorative point of view, of an ornamental framework was seen and promptly

FIG. 24—DRAWN-WORK SAMPLER BY S. W. A.D. 1700.

Mrs C. J. Longman.

followed. The earliest border I have seen is that reproduced in Fig. 25, from a sampler dated 1726, but it is certain that many must exist between that date and 1700, the date upon the sampler in Fig. 24 just referred to. The 1726 border consists of a pattern of trefoils, worked in alternating red and yellow silks, connected by a running stem of a stiff angular character; the device being somewhat akin to the earlier semi-border in Fig. 24.

It is astonishing with what persistency the samplerists followed the designs which they had had handed to them in the "row" samplers, confining their attentions to a few favourites, and repeating them again and again for a hundred and fifty years, and losing, naturally, with each repetition somewhat of the feeling of the original. We give a few examples which show this persistency of certain ideas.

FIG. 25.—BORDER OF MARY LOUNDS'S SAMPLER. A.D. 1726.

The border in Fig. 26 is dated 1735, and presents but little advance from a decorative point of view. It is the production of

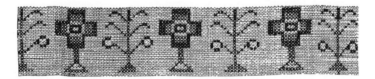

FIG. 26.—BORDER OF MARY HEAVISIDE'S SAMPLER. A.D. 1735.

Mary Heaviside, and is upon an Easter sampler, which bears, besides the verse to the Holy Feast of Easter, the Lord's Prayer

FIG. 27.—BORDER OF ELIZABETH GREENSMITH'S SAMPLER. AGED 10. JULY YE 26, 1737.

and the Belief. The border may possibly typify the Cross and the Tree of Life.

Elizabeth Greensmith's sampler (Fig. 27), worked two years later, in 1737, is more pretentious in form, the body of the work being taken up with a spreading tree, beneath which repose a lion and a leopard. The border consists of an ill-composed and ill-drawn design of yellow tulips, blue-bells, and red roses. The

FIG. 28.—BORDER OF MARGARET KNOWLES'S SAMPLER. AGED 9. A.D. 1738.

stem, which runs through this and almost every subsequent design, is here very feebly arranged ; it is, however, only fair to say that the work is that of a girl in her tenth year.

Margaret Knowles's sampler (Fig. 28), made in the next year —A.D. 1738—is the earliest example I know of the use on a border of that universal favourite the pink, which is oftentimes hardly

FIG. 29.—BORDER TO SAMPLER BY ELIZABETH TURNER. A.D. 1771.

distinguishable from the corn blue-bottle. In the present instance it is, however, flattened almost out of recognition, whilst the design is spoilt by the colossal proportions of the connecting stem. In the second row of the sampler, Fig. 24, it is seen in a much simpler form, and it will also be found in Plate VI.

The remaining illustrations of borders are selected as being

those where the design is well carried out, and as showing how
the types continue. The first (Fig. 29), worked by Elizabeth
Turner in 1771, represents a conventional rose in two aspects;
the second, by Sarah Carr (Fig. 30), in 1809, is founded on the

FIG. 30.—BORDER TO SAMPLER BY SARAH CARR. A.D. 1809.

honeysuckle; whilst the third (Fig. 31) is a delightfully simple
one of wild strawberries that is frequently found in samplers from
the earliest (in Plate II.) onwards. In that from which this
example is taken, worked by Susanna Hayes in 1813, it is most
effective with its pink fruit and green stalks and band. It will

FIG. 31.—BORDER TO SAMPLER BY SUSANNA HAYES. A.D. 1813.

be noticed that it even crossed the Atlantic, for it reappears in
Mr Pennell's American sampler, Plate XIII.

How even the border degenerated as the nineteenth century
advanced may be seen in the monotonous Greek fret used in the
three samplers of the Brontës (Figs. 10, 11, 12), and in that of
Mary Anderson (Fig. 19).

Miscellanea respecting Samplers

Under this heading we group what remains to be said concerning samplers, namely :—

The Age and Sex of Sampler Workers

In modern times samplers have been almost universally the product of children's hands ; but the earliest ones exhibit so much more proficiency that it would seem to have been hardly possible that they could have been worked by those who were not yet in their teens. This supposition is in a way supported by an examination of samplers. Of those prior to the year 1700, I have seen but one in which the age of the maker is mentioned. It reads thus, "Mary Hall is my name and when I was thirteen years of age I ended this in 1662." On the other hand, the rhyme which we quoted at page 50, attached to one in Mrs Longman's possession, which, although undated, is certainly of the seventeenth century, points to it being the work of a grown-up and possibly a married lady.

It is not until we reach the year 1704 that I have found a sampler (Fig. 32) which was the product of a child under ten, namely, that bearing the inscription "Martha Haynes ended her sampler in the 9th year of her age, 1704."

This is quickly followed by one by "Anne Michel, the daughter of John and Sarah Michel ended Nov. the 21 being 11 years of age and in the 3 year of Her Majesti Queen Anne and in the year of ovr Lord 1705."

1740 is the next date upon one worked by Mary Gardner, aged 9 (page 27).

FIG. 32.—SMALL SAMPLER BY MARTHA HAYNES. DATED 1704.
Late in the Author's Collection.

PLATE XVI.

NONE of the Embroideries reproduced in this volume approach this in their imitation of Tapestry, it being a facsimile on a small scale in needlework of a large panel. Its resemblance is increased by the border, which adds considerably to its interest and value. Both Sovereigns are crowned, the King wearing a cloak, a vest and breeches which would appear to be all in one (the latter garnished at the knees with many points), boots with huge tops, and big spurs. On either side of the royal pair stand a chamberlain and a lady of honour. The house in the background points to the Tapestry having been designed by a Netherlander.

PLATE XVI.—TAPESTRY EMBROIDERY. CHARLES I. AND HIS QUEEN. ABOUT 1630.

From 1750 onwards the majority of samplers are endorsed with the age of the child, and the main interest in the endorsements lies in the remarkable proficiency which many of them exhibit, considering the youth of the worker, and in the tender age at which they were wrought. Almost one half of the tiny workers have not reached the space when their years are marked with two figures, and we even have one mite of six producing the piece of needlework reproduced in Fig. 33, and talking of herself as in her prime in the verse set out upon it.

But perhaps the most remarkable achievement is the "goldfinch" sampler illustrated in Plate XII., which was worked by Ann Maria Wiggins at the age of seven.

It is not un-

FIG. 33.—SAMPLER BY SARAH PELHAM, AGED 6.

reasonable to suppose that samplers were on occasions worked by children of both sexes. One's own recollection carries back to canvas and Berlin wool-work having been one way of passing the tedious hours of a wet day. But specimens where the Christian name of a male appears are few and far between, and more often than not they are worked in conjunction with others, which would seem to indicate that they are only there as part and parcel of a list (which is not unusual) of the family. In the sampler illustrated in Fig. 34 the boy's name, Robert Henderson, is in black silk, differing from any of the rest of the lettering, which is perhaps testimony to his having produced it. This sampler shows the perpetuation until 1762 of the form in which rows are the predominant feature. A sampler, formerly in the author's collection, was more clearly that of a boy, being signed Lindsay Duncan, Cuper [*sic*], 1788. Another Scottish one bears the name or names Alex. Peter Isobel Dunbar, whilst a third of the same kind is signed "Mathew was born on April 16, 1764, and sewed this in August, 1774."

The Size of Samplers

The ravages of time and the little value attached to them have probably reduced to very small numbers the tiny samplers such as those which are seen in Figs. 35 and 36, and which must have usually been very infantine efforts. Those illustrated, however, show the progress made by two sisters, Mary and Lydia Johnson, in two years. Presumably Lydia was the elder, and worked the sampler which bears her name and the date 1784. This was copied by her sister Mary in the following year, but in a manner which showed her to be but a tyro with the needle ; nor much advanced in stitchery in the following year, in which she attempted the larger

FIG. 34.—SCOTTISH SAMPLER BY ROBERT HENDERSON. DATED 1762.

PLATE XVIII.

THIS remarkably well-preserved piece of Embroidery represents various incidents in the life of Queen Esther. In the centre the King stretches forth his sceptre to the Queen; in the various corners are portrayed the banquet, the hanging of Haman, and Mordecai and the King. It will be noticed that the King and Queen are likenesses of Charles I. and Henrietta Maria, and the costume is that in vogue towards the end of his reign, when the big boots worn by the men came in for much ridicule, the tops of the King's being "very large and turned down, and the feet two inches too long." The needlework is of the transition period, when a better effect was sought for by appliquéing the faces in satin, outlining the features in silk, and making the hair of the same material. The collars and bows are also added, and the Queen's crown is of pearls, the dais on which the King sits being also sown with them. Size, 16½ × 20½.

PLATE XVIII.—TAPESTRY EMBROIDERY. THE STORY OF QUEEN ESTHER. ABOUT 1630.

FIG. 35.—SMALL SAMPLERS BY MARY JOHNSON.   1785-6.
Author's Collection.

FIG. 36.—SMALL SAMPLERS BY LYDIA JOHNSON.   1784.
Author's Collection.

sampler which bears her name. Lydia, on the other hand, in the undated sampler, but which was probably made in the year 1786, showed progress in everything except the power of adapting the well-known design of a pink to the small sampler on which she was engaged, as to which she clearly could not manage the joining of the pattern at the corners. The originals of these samplers measure from four to six inches in their largest dimensions.

The Place of Origin of Samplers

Collectors, in discussing samplers among themselves, have wondered whether it would be possible to assign differences in construction and material to their having been produced in localities where the characteristic forms and patterns had not permeated. But those specimens which the author has examined, and which by a superscription gave a clue as to their place of origin, certainly afford insufficient foundation for such assumptions. In the first place, samplers so marked are certainly not sufficiently numerous to warrant any opinion being formed on the subject, and, as to those not so marked, the places where they have been found cannot be taken into account as being their birthplaces, as families to whom they have for long belonged may naturally have removed from quite different parts of the kingdom since the samplers were made.

It is surprising how seldom the workers of samplers deemed it necessary to place upon them the name of the district which they inhabited. There are few who followed the example of the girl who describes herself on a sampler dated 1766, thus :—

> "Ann Stanfer is my name
> And England is my nation
> Blackwall is my dwelling place
> And Christ is my salvation."

The only names of places in England recorded on samplers in The Fine Art Society's Exhibition were Chipping Norton, Sudbury, Hawkchurch, and Tottenham, and certain orphan schools or hospitals, such as Cheltenham and Ashby. Curiously enough, the Scottish lassies were more particular in adding their dwelling-place, thus, in the sampler reproduced in Fig. 37, and which is interesting as a survival as late as 1779 of a long sampler, Mary Bayland gives her residence as Perth, and others have been noted at Cupar, Dunbar, and elsewhere in Scotland. It might be expected that these Scottish ones would differ materially from those made far away in the southern parts of the kingdom, but whilst the one shown in Fig. 34 has a certain resemblance and difference from others in the decoration of its lettering, that in Fig. 37 might well have been worked in England, showing that there were no local peculiarities such as we might expect.

It will be seen that two of the American samplers figured here have their localities indicated, namely Miss Damon's school at Boston (Fig. 50) and Brooklyn (Fig. 47).

FIG. 37.—SCOTTISH SAMPLER BY MARY BAYLAND. 1779.

Samplers as Records of National Events

FIG. 38.—SAMPLER BY MARY MINSHULL.
DATED JUNE 29, 1694.

A largely added interest might have been given to samplers had a fashion arisen of lettering them with some historical occurrence which was then stirring the locality, but unfortunately their makers very rarely rose to so much originality. Three rare instances were to be seen in The Fine Art Society's Exhibition. These, curiously enough, came together from different parts of the country—one from Nottingham, a second from Hockwold, Norfolk, and the third from the author's collection in London—but they were worked by two persons only, one by Mary Minshull, and two by Martha Wright. They are all unusual in their form of decoration (as will be seen by that illustrated in Fig. 38), and were practically similar in design, colour, and execution, each having a set of single pinks worked in high relief in the centre of the sampler. Their presence together was certainly a testimony to the all-embracing character of the Exhibition. The inscriptions upon them were as follows :—

(1) "The Prince of Orang landed in the West of England on the 5th of November 1688, and on the 11th April 1689 was crowned King of England, and in the year 1692 the French came to invade England, and a fleet of ships sent by King William drove them from the English seas, and took, sunk, and burned twenty-one of their ships."—Signed "*Martha Wright, March 26th, 1693.*"

(2) "There was an earthquake on the 8 of September 1692 in the City of London, but no hurt tho it caused most part of England to tremble."—Signed "*Mary Minshull.*"

The third was a combination of the two inscriptions.

Nothing of a similar character in work of the eighteenth century has come under my notice, but the Peace of 1802 produced the following lines on a sampler :—

"Past is the storm and o'er the azure sky serenely shines the sun
With every breeze the waving branches nod their kind assent."

ON PEACE

"Hail England's favor'd Monarch : round thy head
Shall Freedom's hand Perennial laurels spread.
Fenc'd by whose sacred leaves the royal brow
Mock'd the vain lightnings aim'd by Gallic foe
Alike in arts and arms illustrious found
Proudly Britannia sits with laurel crown'd
Invasion haunts her rescued Plains no more
And hostile inroads flies her dangerous shore
Where'er her armies march her ensigns Play
Fame points the course and glory leads the way.

*　　*　　*　　*　　*

O Britain with the gifts of Peace thou'rt blest
May thou hereafter have Perpetual rest

And may the blessing still with you remain
Nor cruel war disturb our land again.

"The Definitive Treaty of Peace was signed March 27th 1802 proclaimed
in London April the 29th 1802—Thanksgiving June the 1st 1802.

Mary Ann Crouzet
Dec^{br} 17 1802."

Later samplers gave expression to the universal sympathy
elicited by the death of Queen Charlotte.

Map Samplers

Needlework maps may very properly be classed under the
head of samplers, for they originated in exactly the same way,
namely, as specimens of schoolgirl proficiency, which when taken
home were very lasting memorials of the excellence of that teaching
termed "the use of the globes."

Maps were only the product of the latter half of the eighteenth
century ; at least, none that I have seen go back beyond that
time, the earliest being dated 1777.   Their interest for the most
part is no more than that of a map of a contemporary date ; for
instance, the North America reproduced in Fig. 39 has nothing
whatever in the way of needlework to recommend it, but it shows
what any map would, namely, how little was known at that date
of the Western States or Canada.

A map of Europe in the Exhibition, dated 1809, was a marvellous
specimen of patient proficiency in lettering, every place of note being
wonderfully and minutely sewn in silk.   The executant was Fanny
le Gay, of Rouen.

A map printed on satin or other material was sometimes
worked over, not always as regards all the lettering, but as to the

markings of the degrees of latitude and longitude,[1] and some of the

FIG. 39.—MAP OF NORTH AMERICA BY M.A.K.   1788.

principal names. These have naturally less interest and value as
specimens of needlework than those which are entirely hand

<hr />

[1] A map of Europe, formerly in the author's possession, had the degrees marked
as so many minutes or hours east or west of Clapton !

worked, although for the purposes of geographical reference they were at all events reliable, which is more than can be said for some of the original efforts; as, for instance, that of little Ann

FIG. 40.—MAP OF ENGLAND AND WALES BY ANN BROWN.

Brown, whose map of England and Wales is reproduced (Fig. 40). Starting bravely, her delineation of Northumberland takes her well down the canvas, so that by the time she has reached Newcastle

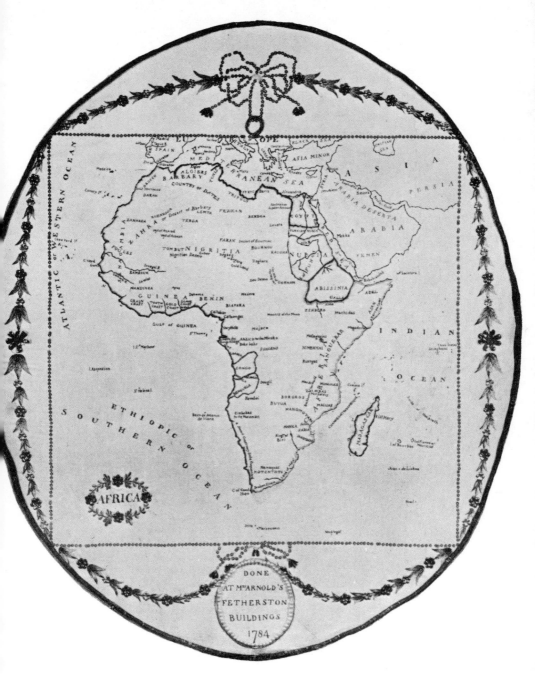

Fig. 41.—Map of Africa. Dated 1784.

PLATE XIX.

WE have here the top of the lid of the best preserved casket it has been our fortune to encounter, the reproduction in no way exaggerating the brilliancy or freshness of the surface. The whole of the embroidery is in high relief, and as the shadows show, much of it is detached from the ground, as for instance the strawberries, the apples on the tree on which the parroquet with his ruffled feathers is seated, and the pink and tulip. For some reason not apparent, the gentleman has two left arms and hands, in each of which he holds a hat. It is possible that the figures may be intended for Abraham and Sarah, the latter with her flock at the well.

PLATE XIX.—LID OF A CASKET.   ABOUT 1660.

she has carried it abreast of Dumfries in Scotland, and Cork in Ireland! Yorkshire is so expansive that it grows downward beyond Exeter and Lundy Island, which last-named places have, however, by some mishap, crept up to the northward of Manchester and Leeds. It is a puzzle to think where the little lassie lived who could consort London with Wainfleet, the River Thames with the Isle of Wight, Lichfield with Portland, or join France to England. Although one would imagine that the dwelling-place of the sempstress would usually be made notable in the map either by large lettering or by more florid colouring, we have not found this to be the case.

The map of Africa (Fig. 41), which is surrounded by a delightful border of spangles, and which seems to have been used as a fire-screen, is interesting now that so much more is known of the continent, for many of the descriptions have undergone considerable change, such as the Grain Coast, Tooth Coast, and Slave Coast, which border on the Gulf of Guinea. The sampler is also noteworthy as having been done at Mrs Arnold's, which was presumably a school in Fetherstone Buildings, High Holborn, hardly the place where one would expect to find a ladies' seminary nowadays.

American Samplers

Tapestry pictures have such a Royalist air about them that it is hardly probable that they found favour with the Puritan damsels of the Stuart reigns, and, consequently, it may be doubted whether the fashion for making them crossed the Atlantic to the New World with the Pilgrim Fathers, or those who followed in their train. Samplers, on the other hand, with their moralities and their seriousness, would seem to be quite akin to the old-fashioned homes

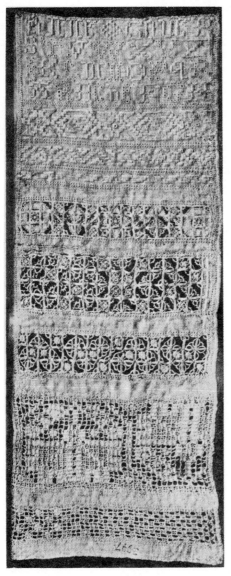

FIG. 42.—DRAWN-WORK SAMPLER BY ANNE GOWER, FIRST WIFE OF GOVR. J. ENDICOTT.

of the New Englanders, and doubtless there must be many specimens hanging in the houses of New England and elsewhere which were produced from designs brought from the Old Country, but over which a breath of native art has passed which imparts to them a distinctive interest and value. Three notable ones, we know, crossed the Atlantic with the early settlers. One, that of Anne Gower (spelled Gover on the sampler), first wife of Governor Endicott (Fig. 42), is now a cherished possession of the Essex Institute, Salem, Massachusetts. As Governor Endicott's wife arrived at Salem in 1628, and died the following year, we have in her sampler the earliest authentic one on record. The inscription of very well-designed and elaborately-worked letters, difficult to distinguish in the photograph, is:—

ANNE ◇ GOVER

S T V W X Y Z

I K L M N O P Q R

A a B C d E F G H

FIG. 43.—SAMPLER OF LORA STANDISH,
DAUGHTER OF THE PILGRIM FATHER,
MILES STANDISH, NOW IN PILGRIM
HALL, PLYMOUTH, U.S.A.

FIG. 44.—SAMPLER BEARING NAMES OF
MILES AND ABIGAIL FLETWOOD.
DATED 1654. *Property of Mrs Frank
Boxer.*

The sampler itself is a beautiful specimen of drawn work, and the lettering is the same colour as the linen. If, as must probably be the case, it was worked by her as a child, it was made in England, and its date may be the end of the first decade of the seventeenth century.

FIG. 45.—SAMPLER BY ABIGAIL RIDGWAY. 1795.

Mr A. D. Drake's Collection.

The second, by Lora Standish, is now in the Pilgrim Hall, Plymouth (Fig. 43). Lora was the daughter of Miles Standish, the Pilgrim Father, who went to Boston in February 1621, and it bears the inscription:—

" Loara Standish is My Name
Lord Guide My Heart that I may do Thy Will
And fill my hands with such convenient Skill
As will conduce to Virtue void of Shame
And I will give the Glory to Thy Name."

FIG. 46.—SAMPLER BY ELIZABETH EASTON.   1795.
Mr A. W. Drake's Collection.

The earliest dated sampler in America of which I have cognisance,
and one which may have been worked in that country, is that

bearing the names of Miles and Abigail Fletwood (Fleetwood?) (Fig. 44). It is dated 1654, and has been owned by the descendants of

FIG. 47.—SAMPLER BY MARIA E. SPALDING. 1815.

Dr I. W. Walker's Collection.

Mrs Henry Quincy since 1750, and is now in the possession of Mrs Frank Boxer of Cambridge, Massachusetts, who has kindly furnished me with particulars concerning it. It bears the following inscription :—

> "In prosperity friends will be plenty,
> But in adversity not one in twenty,"

which, it is thought, may possibly have reference to the reverses of Miles Fletwood and his relationship to Cromwell. It is some-

FIG. 48.—SAMPLER BY MARTHA C. HOOTON. 1827.
Mr A. W. Drake's Collection.

what remarkable for a sampler to bear the names of husband and wife for it necessarily presupposes its having been worked after marriage.

If one may judge from the photographs which collectors in America have sent me, and for which I have to thank Dr James W. Walker of Chicago and Mr A. W. Drake of New York, and those noted in an article on the subject in the

Century Magazine,[1] specimens between the period just named, that is the middle of the seventeenth century and the end of the eighteenth century, are rare. We have but two such figured, each dated 1795, and, as will be seen by the illustrations (Figs. 45 and 46), they are entirely British in character. I am glad, however, to add several interesting specimens of later date from the collections of these gentlemen. Plate XIII belongs to Mr Pennell, the well-known artist and author, and was worked by an ancestress, Martha C. Barton, in 1825. From Mrs Longman's collection I also give (Fig. 51) one, worked in silk on a curious loose canvas, which was obtained by her in Massachusetts, and has the following inscription:—

> "Persevere. Be not weary in well doing.
> Youth in society are like flowers
> Blown in their native bed, 'tis there alone
> Their faculties expand in full bloom
> Shine out, there only reach their proper use.

"Wrought by Lydia J. Cotton. Aged 9 years. Augst 27. 1819. Love learning and improve."

Foreign Samplers

It has been my endeavour in this volume to confine the survey of samplers and embroideries entirely to the production of the English-speaking race, in part because other authors have drawn almost all their material from foreign sources, and the subject is sufficiently ample and interesting without having recourse to them, and also because the collections containing foreign samplers or em-

[1] "Samplers," by Alice Morse Earle.

FIG. 49.—AMERICAN SAMPLER OF THE LAMBORN FAMILY.   1827.

Mr A. W. Drake's Collection.

FIG. 50.—AMERICAN SAMPLER BY ELIZABETH M. FORD.

Dr Jas. W. Walker's Collection.

FIG. 51.—AMERICAN SAMPLER BY LYDIA J. COTTON. DATED 1819.

Mrs C. J. Longman.

broideries are very few, and although they, perhaps, surpass the efforts of our own countrywomen in the variety of their stitches and the proficiency with which they are executed, they take a less important place where interest of subject is the main recommendation.

Nevertheless as the acquisition of them may add an interest to those who never fail on their travels to inspect the contents of every curiosity shop they come across, the following description of them which Mrs C. J. Longman, who possesses a most important collection, has been good enough to furnish, may not be out of place.

" My collection of foreign samplers includes specimens from the following countries: Germany, Holland, Belgium, Denmark, Sweden, France, Switzerland, Italy, Spain, and Portugal, but by far the largest number of my foreign samplers come from Germany, and, next to English ones, the German seem more easy to obtain than those of any other country. In Spain and Portugal there are also a fair number in the market.

" The dated samplers abroad seem to begin at about the same period as in England, namely, the middle of the seventeenth century. The earliest specimens that I possess from these several countries are as follows : Germany, 1674 ; Switzerland, 1675 ; Italy, seventeenth century (undated) ; Spain, early eighteenth century (undated) ; Belgium, 1724 ; Holland, 1726 ; Denmark, 1742 ; France, 1745 ; Portugal, early nineteenth century (undated).

" There are a few marked characteristics which seem to belong to the different countries, which it is interesting to note.

" In the German samplers, the initials of the worker and the date are almost always given, enclosed together, in a little garland or frame ; but I have never seen the name signed in full. I have only once seen a German sampler with an inscription on it ; in that case ' Fur uns geoffert ' is worked above a representation of the Crucifixion.

" The seventeenth-century German samplers are rather small,

and much squarer in shape than English ones of the same date. With the eighteenth century long, narrow ones came in, a quite common size being 44 in. long, by about 10 in. broad, the usual width of the linen; the selvage is left at the top and bottom.

"There is seldom much arrangement in the earlier German samplers. They usually have one alphabet, and various conventional flowers, birds, and other designs scattered over them.

"With the long shape of sampler a more methodical arrangement came in. A typical one is as follows: Lines of alphabets and numerals across the top, some large subjects in the centre, and designs for borders arranged in lines across the bottom.

"The central subjects very often include a representation of the Crucifixion and emblems of the Passion, namely, the crown of thorns, scourge, ladder, nails, hammer, tweezers, sponge, hour-glass, dice, cock. Adam and Eve under the Tree of Knowledge is another favourite subject, and animals such as lions, deer, or parrots frequently occur. One does not often find houses or domestic scenes. One sampler, dated 1771, has a christening depicted on it, which I imagine to be very unusual.

"The borders are very various. In them trefoils, grapes, conventional pinks, roses, pears, and lilies and occasionally deer and birds are worked in; but I have never seen the 'Boxers' or other figures that one finds in the English borders, and I have only one specimen with acorns.

"The earliest German samplers seem to be worked entirely in cross-stitch, beautifully fine, and the same on both sides of the material; the back-stitching so often found on early English ones I have never seen. In the eighteenth century other stitches were sometimes used, and I have one German sampler, dated 1719, which is almost entirely worked in knots. On others some elaborate stitches are shown, which are mostly worked in square patches, and are not made use of for improving the design of the samplers.

"The earliest examples of darned samplers that I have seen come from Germany, and I think that one may give the Germans the credit of inventing them; for, whereas, in England they do not appear much before the end of the eighteenth century, I have a German one dated 1725, and several others from the middle of the same century. The darns on these samplers show every kind of ordinary and damask darning, the material being usually cut away from underneath and the hole entirely filled in. I have never seen German darning worked into designs of flowers, birds and so on, as we see on English darned samplers.

"As in all countries, the colours of the earlier German samplers are the best, but they are in no case striking.

"Dutch samplers seem quite distinct in character from German ones. All those that I have seen are broader than they are long, and they are worked across the material, the selvage coming at the sides, instead of at the top and bottom. They are usually dated, and signed with initials. One of their main characteristics is to have elaborate alphabets worked in two or more colours. The second colour is very often worked round an ordinary letter as a sort of frame or outer edge, and gives it a clumsy, rather grotesque appearance. The Dutch samplers might, as a rule, be described as patchy. Without any obvious arrangement they have houses, ships, people, animals, etc., scattered over them. The stitch used is mainly cross-stitch; but back-stitch, an open kind of satin-stitch, and bird's-eye-stitch are also often seen.

"Belgian samplers, as far as I have seen, approach more nearly to the German in style. I have one, however, dated 1798, which is quite distinct in character. It is 64 in. in length, with a large, bold alphabet of letters over 2 in. long worked on it, such as might be used for marking blankets.

"I have only three specimens of Danish samplers, but they are all remarkable for the great variety of stitches introduced. I have a Danish sampler, and also a Swedish one of about 1800 worked on fine white muslin, both giving patterns of stitches for the 'Töndu' muslin drawn work. These patterns imitate both needlepoint and pillow laces, threads are drawn out one way of the material, the remaining ones being drawn together with a great variety of stitches, so as to follow the intricacies of lace patterns. This work was much used for adorning elbow ruffles, fichues, etc., and it is very like some Indian muslin work, though the stitches are slightly different.

"French samplers, as far as I have seen, are also remarkable for the fineness of the stitches. They are usually dated and signed in full, and often have inscriptions worked on them. One large French map of Europe in my collection has 414 names worked on it in fine cross-stitch, many of them being worked on a single thread of material, which is a fine muslin.

"Swiss samplers show fine work, but a great lack of effect. One dated 1675 has several borders on it, worked in the back-stitch so much used in England at that date.

"From Italy I have no important coloured samplers, but several point-coupé ones. They are undated but belong to the seventeenth century. These samplers show a beauty of design which is rather in contrast to that of English ones of the same kind and date, there being a grace and meaning about the Italian patterns that one seldom finds in English specimens of drawn work, fine as these are. A typical coloured Italian sampler of about 1800 is as follows : The sampler is nearly square, and is divided into three parts. In the upper division a Latin cross is worked at the side, and the rest of the space is filled with two alphabets, numerals, and the name of the worker, but no date. In the second division a cross is worked, and fourteen emblems of the Passion. In the third division are various trees, figures, animals, etc., some local colour being given by an orange and a lemon tree in pots.

"Spain is well represented in my collection. For beauty of colouring and designs I think that it stands far ahead of any other country. Spanish samplers are generally large; they are sometimes square, sometimes long in shape. They are as a rule entirely covered with border patterns, which in the square shape are worked along the four sides parallel to the edge; and which in the long shape runs in lines across the sampler, with a break in the middle, where the border changes to another pattern, thus giving the impression that the sampler is joined up the centre. The patterns of the borders vary a great deal; I have counted thirty different ones on one sampler. They are mostly geometric, and not based on any natural objects, but the designs are so skilfully handled and elaborately worked out as to take away any appearance of stiffness; and in them the prim acorn, bird, or trefoil of the English and German border patterns are never seen. I have one Spanish sampler, dated 1738, of a quite different type to all my others. It is divided into three panels. The top panel is filled with floral designs, the centre with a gorgeous coat of arms, and the lower panel contains a representation of St George and the Dragon.

"The colours used in Spanish samplers are very striking, and their blending in the different borders is very happy and effective. Most of the early specimens are worked almost entirely in satin-stitch, although cross-stitch and back-stitch are also sometimes introduced. The samplers are usually hem-stitched round the edge, and occasionally contain some drawn work. I have one early specimen in which the drawn part is worked over in coloured silks.

"The Spanish samplers that I have seen seldom have the alphabet worked on them, and are rarely dated. On the other hand, they often have the name of the worker signed in full.

"Portugal is only represented in my collection by samplers worked in the nineteenth century; it is therefore hardly fair to compare these specimens with the earlier ones of other countries, for everywhere samplers began to deteriorate in that century. The Portuguese samplers that I possess are eminently commonplace, and can well be described as 'Early Victorian.'

"It must be remembered that my remarks on foreign samplers are based on specimens belonging to the seventeenth and eighteenth centuries. With few exceptions I have not tried to collect modern ones, which approximate much more to each other in the different countries.

"Looking back over this brief survey, and comparing foreign samplers with English, one or two differences at once stand out. The foreign samplers are seldom worked in a pictorial form. They hardly ever, except in France, have verses or texts worked on them. The age of the worker is never given. This is much to be regretted, as in these three things lies much of the personal interest of the English sampler.

"On the other hand, from a practical point of view, if one goes to one's samplers as to pattern-books for good stitches, designs and effects of colour, England no longer takes the first place, and one would turn for these to the samplers of Germany, Scandinavia, Spain, and Italy."

Indian Samplers

Many of the Anglo-Indian mothers who reared and brought up families in the East Indies in the days when the young ones had to pass all their youth in that country, regardless of climatic stress, must have trained their girls in the cult of sampler-making, and the same schooling went on in the seminaries at Calcutta and elsewhere, as we have seen in the specimen illustrated in Fig. 3. I am able to give another illustration (Fig. 52), which is not otherwise remarkable except for the fact that it was worked by a child

FIG. 52.—SAMPLER BY HELEN PRICE. MADE AT KIRKEE, EAST INDIES. DATED 18—.
Late in the Author's Collection.

at Kirkee, and shows how insensibly the European ornament becomes orientalised as it passes under Eastern influence. It is the only sampler in which there is any use made of plain spaces, and even here it is probably only accidental.

Sampler Literature

Although, undoubtedly, much of the ornament upon samplers consists of designs that have been handed down from generation to generation by means of the articles themselves, pattern-books have not been altogether lacking even from early days. They have not, however, rivalled either in quantity or quality those which treat of the sister Art of lace-making, for, so far as is known, early English treatises on the subject are limited to some half a dozen, and these occupy themselves as much with lacework as with embroidery.

The first English book that is known is in reality a foreign one ; it is entitled, " New and Singular Patternes and Workes of Linnen Serving for Patternes to make all sorts of Lace Edginges and Cut Workes. Newly invented for the profite and contentment of Ladies, Gentilwomen and others that are desireous of this Art. By Vincentio. Printed by John Wolfe 1591." We have not been able to find a copy, and therefore can do no more than chronicle its existence.

A volume upon which needleworkers of the seventeenth century must have relied much more largely for their ideas was published in its early years under the title of " The Needle's Excellency. A New Booke wherein are divers admirable workes wrought with the needle. Newly invented and cut in copper for the pleasure and profit of the industrious. Printed for James Boler, and are to be sold at the Syne of the Marigold in Paules Churchyard." This treatise went to twelve editions at least, but, nevertheless, is very rare. The twelfth, "enlarged with divers newe workes, needleworkes, purles, and others never before printed. 1640," is to be found in the British Museum Library, but even that copy has suffered considerably from usage, for many plates are missing, and few are in consecutive order. The title-page consists of an elaborate copper plate, in which are to be seen Wisdom, Industrie, and Follie; Industrie, seated in the middle under a tree with a formal garden behind her, is showing Follie, who is decked out in gorgeous Elizabethan costume, her work, and Follie is lifting her hands in astonishment at it. Following the title-page comes a lengthy poem by Taylor, the Water Poet, upon the subject of needlework. So far as one can judge from the samplers of the period, the designs for needlework in the book, which consist of formal borders, have been very seldom copied, but some for drawn work undoubtedly have a close resemblance to those which we see in existing pieces. Another book, which I have been unable to find in the Museum, is described as " Patternes of Cut Workes newly invented and never published before : Also Sundry Sorts of Spots, as Flowers, Birdes, and Fishes, etc., which will fitly serve to be wrought, some with gould, some with silke, and some with creuell in coullers ; or otherwise, at your pleasure."

From "The Needle's Excellency" we have many clues as to needlework in the early seventeenth century. First of all, as to the articles for which samplers would be required, the following are mentioned : "handkerchiefs, table cloathes for parloures or for halls, sheetes, towels, napkins, pillow beares." Then as to the objects which were delineated on embroideries, it states that :—

> "In clothes of Arras I have often seene
> Men's figured counterfeits so like have beene
> That if the parties selfe had been in place
> Yet Art would vie with nature for the grace."

Again,

> " Flowers, Plants and Fishes,
> Beasts, Birds, Flyes and Bees,
> Hills, Dales, Plains, Pastures,
> Skies, Seas, Rivers, Trees,
> There's nothing ne'er at hand or farthest sought
> But with the needle may be shap'd and wrought."

It would seem from the foregoing that the volumes would be of more profit to the worker of embroidered pictures than to sampler-makers, and this was no doubt the case ; for when the former went out of fashion, the books dealing with the subject disappeared too, and nothing further of any note was published, except in the beginning of the last century, when the National Schools were furnished with manuals which dealt more with plain sewing than with decorative needlework.

The Last of the Samplers

I can hardly close my remarks upon the entertaining subject, the elucidation of and material for which has filled many spare hours, without a word of regret at having to pen the elegy of the sampler.

It may be said that even so long ago as the era of the *Spectator* there were those who sounded its death knell, and who considered that the days when a lady crowded a thousand graces on to the surface of a garter were gone for ever. For did it not go to the heart of one of Mr Spectator's correspondents to see a couple of idle flirts sipping their tea for a whole afternoon, in a room hung round with the industry of their great-grandmothers, and did he not implore that potentate to take the laudable mystery of embroidery into his serious consideration ?

But even then there were matrons who upheld the craft, and of whom an epitaph could be written that "she wrought the whole Bible in tapestry, and died in a good old age after having covered three hundred yards of wall in the Mansion House." Besides, the samplers themselves show that the industry, if not the Art, continued all through that century and for at least half of the nineteenth.

The decadence of the sampler has never been more tenderly or pathetically dealt with than in the description given of the dame's school in the sketch entitled "Lucy," in Miss Mitford's "Our Village."[1]

. . . There are seven girls now in the school working samplers to be framed. "Such a waste of silk, and time, and trouble!" I said to Mrs Smith, and Mrs Smith said to me. Then she recounted the whole battle of the samplers, and her defeat; and then she sent for one which, in spite of her declaration that her girls never finished anything, was quite completed (probably with a good deal of her assistance), and of which, notwithstanding her rational objection to its uselessness, Lucy was not a little proud. She held it up with great delight, pointed out all the beauties, selected her own favourite parts, especially a certain square rosebud, and the landscape at the bottom; and finally pinned it against the wall, to show the effect that it would have when framed. Really, that sampler was a superb thing in its way. First came a plain pink border; then a green border, zig-zag; then a crimson, wavy; then a brown, of a different and more complicated zig-zag; then the alphabet, great and small, in every colour of the rainbow, followed by a row of figures, flanked on one side by a flower, name unknown, tulip, poppy, lily—something orange or scarlet, or orange-scarlet; on the other by the famous rosebud, then divers sentences, religious and moral;—Lucy was quite provoked with me for not being able to read them; I daresay she thought in her heart that I was as stupid as any of her scholars; but never was MS. so illegible, not even my own, as the print-work of that sampler;—then last and finest, the landscape, in all its glory. It occupied the whole narrow line at the bottom, and was composed with great regularity. In the centre was a house of a bright scarlet, with yellow windows, a green door, and a blue roof: on one side, a man with a dog; on the other, a woman with a cat—this is Lucy's information; I should never have guessed that there was any difference, except in colour, between the man and the woman, the dog and the cat; they were in form, height, and size, alike to a thread, the man grey,

---

[1] It first appeared in the *Lady's Magazine*, 1819, and in the first collected edition, 1824, Vol. I. pp. 67, 68; also in Bohn's Classics, 1852, pp. 138, 139.

FIG. 53.—BEADWORK SAMPLER BY JANE MILLS. 19TH CENTURY.
Late in the Author's Collection.

NOTE.—The only modern sampler in The Fine Art Society's Exhibition in which beadwork was employed. This is the more remarkable as it apparently dates from about the period when beadwork was so much in fashion for purses, etc. As we shall see in our illustrations of pictures in imitation of tapestry (Plate XXI.), beadwork was very common in the seventeenth century, but we have not seen a single specimen of this material dated in the eighteenth century, unless it be this one, which we place at the end of the eighteenth or the beginning of the nineteenth century.

the woman pink, his attendant white, and hers black.   Next to these figures, on either side, rose two fir-trees from two red flower-pots, nice little round bushes of a bright green or intermixed with brown stitches, which Lucy explained, not to me—" Don't you see the fir-cones, sir?   Don't you remember how fond she used to be of picking them up in her little basket at the dear old place?   Poor thing, I thought of her all the time that I was working them!   Don't you like the fir-cones?"—After this, I looked at the landscape almost as lovingly as Lucy herself.

It has been prophesied that :—

> "Untill the world be quite dissolv'd and past
> So long at least the needles use shall last."

I trow not, if for "use" the word "Art" may be substituted.

It is true that recent International Exhibitions have included some marvellous specimens of adroitness in needlework, such, for instance, as the wonders from Japan ; but these *tours de force*, and even the skilled productions from English schools, as, for instance, "The Royal School of Art Needlework," and which endeavour fitfully to stir up the dying embers of what was once so congenial an employment to womankind, are no indications of any possibility of needlework regaining its hold on either the classes or the masses.

Samplers can never again be a necessity whereby to teach the young idea, and every year that passes will relegate them more and more into the category of interesting examples of a bygone and forgotten industry.

One sampler dated within the last half century finds a place in this book, but it is indeed a degraded object, and is included here to show to what the fashion had come in the Victorian era, an era notable for huge sums being expended on Art schools, and over a million children receiving Art instruction at the nation's expense. The sampler is dated 1881, and was the work of a lady of seventeen years of age.   The groundwork is a common handkerchief, the young needlewoman evidently considering that its puce-coloured printed border was a better design than any she could invent.   It

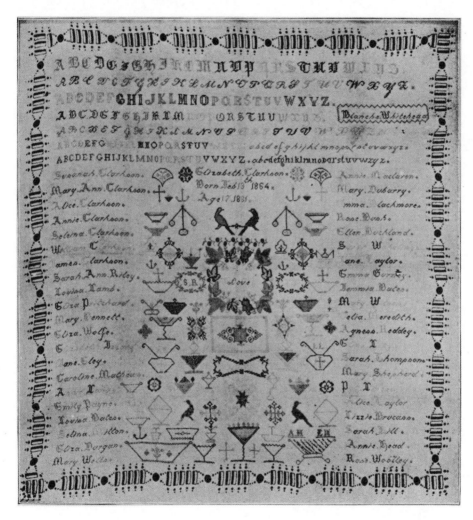

FIG. 54.—SAMPLER BY ELIZABETH CLARKSON. 1881.
Author's Collection.

was produced at a school, for there are broidered upon it the names of thirty-five other girls, besides seven bearing her own patronymic. As will be seen by the reproduction (Fig. 54), it is adorned with no less than nine alphabets, not one of which contains an artistic form of lettering. As to the ornament, the cross and anchor hustle the pawnbroker's golden balls, and formless leaves surround the single word "Love," all that the maker's invention could supply of sentimentality. This is apparently the best that the deft fingers of Art-taught girlhood could then produce. The flash in the pan that, round about the date of its creation, was leading to the production of the "chairback" in crewels, collapsed before machine-made imitations, and well it might when even a knowledge of how to stitch an initial is unnecessary, as we can obtain by return of post from Coventry, at the price of a shilling or so a hundred, a roll of our names in red, machine-worked, lettering. Truly it seems as if any use for needlework in the future will be relegated to an occasional spasmodic effort, such as when war confronts us and our soldiers are supposed to be in need of a hundred thousand nightcaps or mufflers.

The decay of needlework amongst the children of the middle classes may perhaps be counterbalanced by other useful employments, but undoubtedly with those of a lower stratum of society the lack of it has simply resulted in their filling the blank with the perusal of a cheap literature, productive of nothing that is beneficial either to mind or body.

FIG. 55.—EMBROIDERED GLOVE. EARLY 17TH CENTURY.
Formerly in the Author's Collection.

PART II

Embroideries in the Manner of Tapestry Pictures

THE Exhibition at The Fine Art Society's included, besides samplers, a gallery containing embroideries, the like of which had not previously been seen together, and as to the history of which text-books were altogether silent.   Exhibited collectively, they not only formed a most interesting and unusual whole, but they were clearly the result of a widespread fashion.   Specimens were forthcoming in considerable numbers, and were regarded by their owners with a proper appreciation of their archæological value, but with a diffidence as to their history and origin which was not surprising.   Under these circumstances it seemed that the occasion of their being brought together should not be lost, and that some illustration of representative specimens, some setting down of any deductions which might be arrived at from their examination and comparison, and some collation of the information which was supplied by their owners should be taken in hand.

It was, however, at the outset a matter of no little trouble to find a title which, while it identified and included them, yet excluded those that it was felt necessary to omit. Had a shortened phrase, such as "Embroidered Pictures," been selected, readers would reasonably have expected to find a survey of that large class of embroideries, now somewhat in vogue, which imitate the coloured engravings of the late eighteenth century, and, perhaps, even of the Berlin wool-work travesties of Landseer and his contemporaries. "Stuart Embroidered Pictures," or "Seventeenth-Century Embroidered Pictures," would have better served the purpose were it not that some of the examples precede, and some follow, the period covered by either. Besides, some pieces are not pictures, whilst others, though pictorial in subject, are covers to caskets, etc.

The majority, however, have this in common, that they represent a phase of embroidery which, curiously enough, originated contemporaneously with the introduction of the manufacture of tapestry into this country, became popular concurrently with it, and passed out of favour when the production of that textile ceased in England for lack of support. It was this relationship, which I shall shortly proceed to establish, that decided the title which is found at the heading of this part.

In endeavouring to trace the origin of these embroideries I have been, curiously enough, confronted with exactly the same difficulties that I encountered in dealing with samplers, namely :—

1. The industry has no apparent infancy, all the pieces having the same matured appearance.

2. No specimen earlier than the reign of Elizabeth has come

under my notice. This does not arise from the decay inseparable from the life of a fairly perishable article, for amongst the earliest specimens may be counted the best preserved; besides, similar work, as, for instance, the embroidery of book covers which was subjected to harder usage, extends for centuries further back.

It is for these reasons that I am disposed to attach importance to the theory that the fashion originated with the introduction into England of tapestry, that, like tapestry, it quickly sprang into vogue, and like that article as quickly died out, having for some half a century been an agreeable occupation for deft hands to busy themselves about.

If we glance for a moment at the history of tapestry in this country, it will be seen how entirely it mirrors that of the embroideries under notice. Tapestry, as an English manufacture, and tapestry of sufficient amount to afford opportunities to any but a few to imitate it, can hardly be said to have existed in this country prior to the seventeenth century. In the king's palaces, and in those of his wealthy ministers and nobles, this form of decoration was undoubtedly in use in remote times, perhaps as early as in those of other nations, but small interest was taken in its production in comparison with that by foreign countries, even those so contiguous as France and the Netherlands. In fact, until the close of the sixteenth century, but one manufactory is known to have existed in England, namely, that of Burcheston, founded towards the end of the reign of Henry VIII. by William Sheldon, styled "The only author and beginner of tapestry, within this realm." It was not until the year 1620 that James I., stimulated by the example of Henri IV., enlisted in his service a number of Flemish workmen and established at Mortlake the factory which quickly attained to a success which was only rivalled by that of the Gobelins. The industry on the banks of the Thames developed rapidly, and secured European recognition, thanks to the extreme interest taken in it by James I., and still more so by Charles I., aided, as he was, by the invaluable co-operation of Rubens and Vandyck. Tapestry made under royal patronage quickly became the fashion and hobby, and although under the Commonwealth its continuance was threatened, it received fresh favours and subventions under Charles II., at the end of whose reign, however, it not only declined, but practically ceased to exist.

It can readily be understood that the prevalence of such a fashion, coinciding with a period when every lady in the land was an adept with her needle, would stimulate many to imitate on a smaller scale the famed productions of the loom, for nothing would better accord with the tapestry-covered walls, than cushions for the oaken chairs, or pictures or mirrors for panelled walls, worked in the same materials. Hence it is probable that all the earlier embroideries were in imitation of tapestry, and worked only in stitches which resembled those of the loom, and that the pieces where we find varieties of stitches introduced, as well as figures, dresses, and animals in relief, are subsequent variations and fancied improvements on the original idea.[1] This is borne out by an examination of dated pieces, none of those bearing these additions being contemporaneous with the introduction of the tapestry industry, whilst only those having a plain surface are found amongst the earliest specimens.[2]

[1] These latter, with their figures standing out in relief, could never have been used for cushions, and can only have been employed as pictures.

[2] The difficulty of assigning a close date to tapestry embroideries is a considerable one, for dress is practically the only guide, and this is by no means a reliable one, for a design may well have been taken from a piece dated half a century previously, as, for instance, when the marriage of Charles I. is portrayed on an embroidery bearing date 1649, the year of his death. Those, therefore, which have a genuine date have this value, that they can only represent a phase of art or a subject coeval with, or precedent to, that date. Hence the importance of the pieces illustrated in Fig. 68 and in Fig. 60, dated six years later.

Embroidery probably reached the zenith of its popularity in the late sixteenth century. It was then of so much importance that Queen Elizabeth granted a charter of incorporation to an Embroiderers' Company who had a hall in Gutter Lane. In order to encourage the pursuit foreign embroideries were in this and the following reigns considered to be contraband, but this protection, instead of improving, practically rang the death knell of the Art.

It will be seen from the foregoing that these little embroideries have an abiding interest of a threefold nature. First that arising out of the subjects that are depicted thereon, and which, though limited in range, present considerable differences when compared one with another, quite sufficient to make them individual in character. Next they afford, upon examination, a large amount of historical material, some of it of a valuable kind, concerning the fashions and cranks of the time, material which has not hitherto met with recognition such as it deserves. Lastly, they are admirable specimens of needlework, and in this are quite as note-worthy as samplers, a single piece often containing as many varieties of clever stitches as may be found in a dozen samplers. All that concerns them on this last-named account will be found in the section devoted to "Stitchery." I will, therefore, proceed to examine them collectively from the two first points of view, leaving any remarks which they may separately call for to the notes which accompany the reproductions.

The Subjects of Tapestry Embroideries

These are, as we have noted, somewhat limited as regards range, and somewhat limited within that range. This is, perhaps, even more so than in the case of the parent tapestries, for whilst they frequently travel into the realms of mythology, the reverse is the case with the embroidered pictures. In the royal palaces of Henry VIII. we find the Tales of Thebes and Troy, the Life and Adventures of Hercules, and of Jupiter and Juno, depicted in tapestry more often, perhaps, than sacred subjects, but this is not so with our little pictures. For instance, there were but two profane subjects in the Embroidery Exhibition, "Orpheus charming the animals with his lute," and the "Judgment of Paris" (Fig. 56); whereas there were at least half a dozen of "Esther and Ahasuerus," and more than one "Susannah and the Elders," "Adam and Eve," "Abraham and Hagar," "Joseph and Potiphar," "David and Abigail," "Queen of Sheba," and "Jehu and Jezebel."

Our first parents naturally afforded one of the earliest Biblical subjects for tapestry. Thus a description of a manor house in King John's time states that in the corner of a certain apartment stood a bed, the tapestry of which was enwrought with gaudy colours representing Adam and Eve in the Garden of Eden, and we read in a fifteenth-century poem by H. Bradshaw, concerning the tapestry in the Abbey of Ely, that :—

"The storye of Adam there was goodly wrought
And of his wyfe Eve, bytwene them the serpente."

In embroidered pictures the working of the nude figures on a necessarily much smaller scale would appear to have been a difficulty it was hard to contend with, and we consequently find the subject treated for the most part rather from the point of view of the animals to be introduced than from that of our first parents.

Curiously enough, Adam and Eve came to the front again as a most popular subject in samplers in the eighteenth and nineteenth centuries, at a time when a knowledge of the draughtsmanship of the human figure appeared to be even slighter than heretofore. Consequently, they were usually of the most primitive character, standing on either side of a Tree of Knowledge, from which depends the serpent.

Passing onwards in Bible history we find in tapestry embroideries several incidents in the life of Abraham.   First the entertainment of

Fig. 56.—The Judgment of Paris.   About 1630.

Late in the Author's Collection.

the angels and the promise made to him ; next the casting forth of Hagar and Ishmael (Plate XV.), oft repeated, perhaps, because of the many incidents in the story capable of illustration ; then the offering up of Isaac, as illustrated in Plate IV. "Moses in the Bullrushes" (Fig. 57) completes the illustrations from the Pentateuch.

Few other subjects are met with until we reach the life of David as pictured in "David and Goliath" and "David and Abigail." To these follow the visit of the Queen of Sheba to Solomon, and the judgment of that ruler. But the most popular subject of all would seem to be the episode of Queen Esther and King Ahasuerus (Plate XVIII.), from which Mordecai sitting in the King's Gate, Esther adventuring on the King's favour, the banquet to Haman, and his end on the gallows, furnished delightfully sensational episodes, although the main reason for its frequency doubtless depended upon its offering an opportunity of honouring the reigning kings and queens by figuring them as the great monarch Ahasuerus and his beautiful consort, a reason also for the frequent selection of Solomon and the Queen of Sheba. The only incident subsequent to this is one hardly to be expected, namely, "Susannah and the Elders," from the Apocrypha (Plate XIV.). The New Testament, curiously enough, seems to have received but scant attention, even the birth of Christ being but seldom illustrated.

If space permitted it would be a matter of interest to trace the reasons for this unexpectedness of subject. It may have arisen from the fact that the English at this time were "the people of one book, and that book the Bible." It is, however, more readily conceivable that the selection was a survival of the times when the mainstay of all the Arts was the Church, and the majority of the work, all the world over, was produced in its service, and therefore naturally was imbued with a religious flavouring.

Again, the pieces being in imitation of tapestries, the subjects would naturally follow those figured thereon. Now we find, curiously enough, in the "Story of Tapestrys in the Royal Palaces of Henry VIII.," that whilst there were a few such subjects as "Jupiter and Juno," and "Thebes and Troy," the majority were the following: In the Tower of London, "Esther and Ahasuerus"; in Durham Palace, "Esther" and "Susannah"; in Cardinal Wolsey's Palace, the "Petition of Esther," the "Honouring of Mordecai," and the "History of Susannah and the Elders," bordered with the Cardinal's arms, subjects identical with those represented in our little embroidered pictures.

It has been claimed for many of these pieces that they are the product of those prolific workers the nuns of Little Gidding, but the assertion rests on as little basis as does that which ascribes all the embroidered book covers to the same origin. The subjects, although sacred in character, are too mundane in habit to render it at all probable that they were worked in the seclusion of a country nunnery.

The foreign origin of the tapestries (even those which were manufactured in England being made and designed by foreigners) accounts for the foreign flavour which pervades their backgrounds and accessories. It has, consequently, been asserted that the inspiration of these embroidery pictures is also foreign, the assertion being based on the fact that the buildings are for the most part of Teutonic design. This is not my opinion. The buildings, it is true, for the most part assume a Flemish or German air, but this is probably due to the reason given at the commencement of this paragraph. It might, with equal force, be held that the pieces are Italian in their origin, as their foregrounds, as we shall presently show, largely affect that style. That either of these suppositions is correct is negatived by the thoroughly English contemporary costume that apparels the principal figures, which also proves that the majority of the pieces were in the main original conceptions, the designers following in the footsteps of their forerunners from the times of Greece downwards, and clothing their puppets, no matter to what age they appertained, in the contemporary dress of their own country. This brings us to the most interesting feature of these little pictures, namely, their value as mirrors of fashion.

Tapestry Embroideries as Mirrors of Fashion

In this respect they are hardly inferior, as illustrations, to the pictures of Vandyck or the engravings of Hollar; whilst, as sidelights to horticultural pursuits under the Stuart kings, and of the flowers which were then affected, they are perhaps more reliable authorities than the Herbals from whence it has been erroneously asserted that they derived their information. In these respects their value has been entirely overlooked. Authorities on dress go to obscure engravings, or to the brasses or sculptural effigies in our churches, for examples, which have, in every instance, been designed by a man unversed in the intricacies of dressmaking. They have failed to recognise the fact that these embroideries are the product of hands which very certainly knew the cut of every garment, and the intricacy of every bow, knot, and point, and which would take a pride in rendering them not only with accuracy, but in the latest mode. It was probably due to this desire to make their work complete mirrors of fashion, that the embroideresses gave up illustrating the figure in the flat, and stuffed it out like a puppet, upon which each portion of the dress might be superimposed. An illustration of this may be seen in the reproduction on a large scale, in the text of Part III., of some of the figures from the piece of embroidery illustrated in Plate XXIII.[1]

As Sir James Linton, an eminent authority upon the dress of the period under review, has pointed out, these embroideries bear upon their face an impress of truth, for they usually, in the same picture, illustrate fashions extending over a considerable period of

[1] Mr Davenport considers that this rounded, padded work is a caricature of the raised embroidery of the *opus Anglicanum*, and that the earliest specimens of it are to be found at Coire, Zurich, and Munich.

time.   This, instead of being an inaccuracy, is unimpeachable evidence as to their correctness, for the fact is usually overlooked that in those times a man (and a woman also) almost invariably wore, throughout life, the costume of his early manhood, and that in such a piece as that illustrated in Plate XIV. it is quite accurate to represent the old men in the costume of the reign of James I., and the young women in that of Charles I.

The repetition, amounting almost to monotony, in the subjects of these tapestry pieces has been urged against them, but the force of this depreciation is considerably lessened if this question of costume and accessories is taken into account, for a comparison even of the few pieces which are illustrated here will show how much variety is afforded in matters of dress, even if that of a single individual, such as Charles I., is selected for study, although in the case of a royal personage, such as the king, it would only be natural if there was a sameness of costume.   He may probably never have been seen by the embroiderer, who would consequently dress him from some picture or engraving.   But even here the differences are many and interesting.[1]

They may therefore be deemed worthy of further examination than is usually given them, and this we have accorded in the description attached to each.   We embody, however, an instance here as it is not only an apt illustration of the use of these little pictures as illustrations of dress, but of how their age may be thereby ascertained.   The work in question belongs to Lady Middleton, is illustrated in Fig. 57, and its frame bears an inscrip-

---

[1] The fondness for decking the dress with pearls is quaintly portrayed in these pictures, where they are imitated by seed pearls.   As to these there is an interesting extract extant, from the inventory of St James's House, nigh Westminster, in 1549, wherein among the items is one of "a table [or picture] whereon is a man holding a sword in one hand and a sceptre in the other, of needlework, prettily garnished with seed pearls."

FIG. 57.—TAPESTRY EMBROIDERY. THE FINDING OF MOSES. ABOUT 1640.

Lady Middleton.

tion that it dates from the sixteenth century. The condition of the needlework, and the stitches employed, might well lead to this supposition, but the dress of the attendant to the left of the picture almost exactly corresponds with that on the effigy of one Dorothy Strutt, whose monument is dated 1641. The hair flows freely on the shoulders, but is combed back from the forehead ; it is bunched behind, and from this descends a long coverchief which falls like a mantle ; the sleeves are wide at the top, but confined at the wrist ; a kerchief covers the bust, whilst the gown pulled in at the waist sets fully all round. It will be noted that the chimneys of the house in the background emit volumes of black smoke, a tribute to the Wallsend coal which came only into general use in the early seventeenth century. The greater part of the strong darks in this picture are due to the silk having been painted with a kind of bitumen, which has eaten away the groundwork wherever it has come into contact with it.

The frequent selection of royal personages for illustration is one of the features of the industry, and is probably accounted for by the majority of the workers being persons in the higher walks of life, to whom the divine right of kings and devotion to the Crown were very present matters in those troublous times. It will be further noted that the only pre-Stuart embroideries which are reproduced here (*Frontispiece*, and the covering for a book [Fig. 58]) deal with them.

As I have stated, yet another value attaches to these tapestry embroideries, namely, as illustrations of the fashions in horticulture under the Stuarts. Those who take an interest in gardening will not be slow to recognise this, and they may even carry that interest beyond this Stuart work to the samplers, whereon instances are not wanting of the formal gardening which came over from Holland with King William, and continued under the House of Hanover.

In the embroideries we see repeated again and again the hold

that Italian gardening had obtained in this country at the time
when they were produced, owing to the grafting of ideas carried
from the age of mediæval Art. Note, for instance, the importance

FIG. 58.—PORTION OF A BOOK COVER.   16TH CENTURY.

Author's Collection.

attached to the fountain, which Hertzner, a German, who travelled
through England at the end of the sixteenth century, remarked
upon as being such a feature in gardens. The many columns and
pyramids of marble and fountains of springing water to which he

FIG. 59.—PURL AND APPLIED EMBROIDERY. LADY WITH A RABBIT. ABOUT 1630.
Formerly in the Author's Collection.

An illustration of purl work, the whole of the smaller decorations being in tarnished silver thread sewn upon the original satin. The figure in the centre with a rabbit on her knees, as well as the other flowers and birds, are appliquéd, and are in very fine coloured silks. The date of the piece is, judging from the costume, the early part of the reign of Charles I.

PLATE XX.

WE have here the true imitation of Tapestry as regards stitch, but not so as regards composition, for it is seldom that in Tapestry we find such a lack of proportion as exists in this case between figures and accessories, tulips and carnations standing breast - high, and butterflies larger than human heads. The harpy, which appears on the lower portion of the lid, is an exceptional form of decoration. The backs of caskets are always the least faded portions, as they have been less exposed to the sun and light ; such is the case here, although the whole is in a fine state of preservation. It is one of the few dated pieces in existence, being signed " A. K.," 1657.

PLATE XX.—BACK OF CASKET IN TAPESTRY EMBROIDERY. SIGNED A. K., 1657.

Mrs Percy Macquoid.

alludes are repeated again and again in tapestry pictures. The
pools of fish which are also found in embroideries of the time
were a common feature of the gardens. We read that "A fayre
garden always contained a poole of fysshe if the poole be clene
kept." (Plate XVIII., Fig. 64, and Fig. 68.) The garden also
had green galleries or pergolas formed of light poles overgrown
with roses red and white. These are illustrated in Plate XIV.
The little Noah's Ark trees did not originate in the brain of the
sampler designer, but were actualities which he saw in the garden of
the time, being as old as the Romans, who employed a topiarius
or pleacher, whose sole business was the cutting of trees into fantastic
shapes. This practice was in full swing in Italy in the fifteenth
century, and was familiarised in England by the "Hypnerotomachia
Poliphili," published in 1592, although this book did not introduce it,
for Bacon in his essay on "Gardens" says that the art of pleaching
was already well known and practised in England. They are
quite common objects on the samplers of the eighteenth century,
when the cult was increasingly fostered, William and Mary having
brought over the Dutch fashion of cutting everything into queer
little trifles. An illustration in Worlidge's "Art of Gardening"
might almost be a reproduction of the sampler of 1761 (Plate IX.)
with its trees all set in absolutely similar order and size. This
style, it may be remembered, was doomed upon the advent of
Capability Brown with his attempts at chastening and polishing,
but not reforming, the living landscape.

The embroidered pictures are also interesting as showing the
flowers which found a place in the parterres of English
gardens. A nosegay garden at the beginning of the seventeenth century consisted, we read, of "gillyflowers, marigolds,
lilies, and daffodils, with such strange flowers as hyacinths,
narcissus, also the. red, damaske, velvet, and double province
rose, double and single white rose, the fair and sweet scenting

woodbind, double and single, the violet nothing behind the rose for smelling sweetly."

Figs. 59 and 60 show many of these flowers naturally disposed, as an examination of the samplers of the period displays almost all of them in a decorative form.

A curious feature of these little pictures is the fondness of their makers for introducing grubs of all kinds. This was not altogether fortuitous, or done simply to fill a void, for some of them were certainly as much emblems as the lion and unicorn. The caterpillar, for instance, was a badge of Charles I.

It speaks somewhat for the difficulty of imitating these little pictures, that although their price has increased since this book was first published, from a moderate to a high figure, there are as yet few spurious or much restored pieces on the market, and the same remark may apply to samplers.

FIG. 60.—EMBROIDERY PICTURE. CHARLES I. AND HIS QUEEN. DATED 1663.

Lord Montagu.

This picture is signed "K.B.," and bears the date 1663, and is, through its composition and subject, of much interest. The king and queen stand under an elaborate tent, on the canopy of which is emblazoned the Royal Arms, the rose and the thistle, in heavy gold and silver bullion. The robes of both their majesties are ornamented with coloured flowers in a heavy silver silver tissue. The king is crowned and has an ermine cloak, and his spurred white boots have pink heels.

PLATE XXIV.

DARNING Samplers of unpretentious form date back a long way, but those where they were conjoined to decoration, as in the specimens reproduced here, appeared to cluster round the end of the eighteenth century. Not only are a variety of stitches of a most intricate kind set out on them, but they are done in gay colours, and any monotony is averted by delicately conceived borderings. Whilst "Darning Samplers" cannot be considered as rare, they certainly are not often met with in fine condition. They are a standing testimony to the assiduity and dexterity of our grandparents in the reparation of their household napery.

PLATE XXIV.—DARNING SAMPLER. 1788.

Fig. 61.—Hollie-Point Lace from Top of Christening Cap. 1774.

Formerly in the Author's Collection.

PART III

I.—Stitchery of Pictures in Imitation of Tapestry and the Like

"Tent-worke, Rais'd-worke, Laid-worke, Froste-worke, Net-worke,
Most curious Purles or rare Italian Cut-worke,
Fine Ferne-stitch, Finny-stitch, New-stitch, and Chain-stitch,
Brave Bred-stitch, Fisher-stitch, Irish-stitch, and Queen-stitch,
The Spanish-stitch, Rosemary-stitch, and Morose-stitch,
The Smarting Whip-stitch, Back-stitch, and the Cross-stitch.
All these are good, and these we must allow,
And these are everywhere in practise now."

The Needle's Excellency.—John Taylor.

A WRITER on the interesting subject of the stitchery of embroidered pictures and their allies, is confronted at the outset with a serious difficulty in the almost hopeless confusion which exists as to the proper nomenclature of stitches.

It is hardly too much to say that nearly every stitch has something like half a dozen different names, the result of re-invention or revival by succeeding generations, while to add to the trouble some authorities have assigned ancient names to certain stitches on what appears to be wholly insufficient evidence of identity.

That stitches known as *opus Anglicanum, opus plumarium, opus peclinum,* and so on, were used in embroidery as far back as the thirteenth and fourteenth centuries, is proved by ancient deeds and inventories, but what these stitches actually were we have no means of deciding with any degree of certainty.

We shall, therefore, in these notes describe the stitches under the names by which they are most commonly known, or which seem to describe them most clearly.

Background–Stitches

When the backgrounds of pictures in raised or stump embroidery are not of silk or satin left more or less visible, they are usually worked in one or other of the innumerable varieties of cushion-stitch, so-called, it is said, because it was first introduced in the embroidering of church kneeling-cushions. Foremost among these ground-stitches comes tent-stitch, in which the flat embroidered pictures of a slightly earlier period are entirely executed. Tent-stitch is the first half of the familiar cross-stitch, but is taken over a single thread only, all the rows of stitches sloping the same way as a rule, although occasionally certain desired effects of light and shade are produced by reversing the direction of the stitches in portions of the work. An admirable example of evenly worked tent-stitch is shown in Plate XV., although here, of course, it is not a purely background-stitch, as it is adopted for the whole of the work.

Another commonly used grounding-stitch is that known in

modern times as tapestry or Gobelin-stitch. This is not infrequently confused with tent-stitch, which it much resembles, save that it is two threads in height, but one only in breadth.

Next in order of importance to these two stitches come the perfectly upright ones, which, arranged in a score of different ways, have been christened by an equal number of names. An effective kind, used for the background of many Stuart pictures,

FIG. 62.—CUSHION-STITCH BACKGROUND; EMBROIDERED BOOK COVER, DATED 1703.

consists of a series of the short perpendicular stitches, arranged in a zig-zag or chevron pattern, each row fitting into that above it. This particular stitch, or rather group of stitches, has been named *opus pulvinarium*, but its claim to the title does not seem very well supported. Other and more modern names are Florentine and Hungary-stitch. A neat and pretty cushion-stitch is shown in the background of Fig. 62 on an enlarged scale. This is taken from a quaint little needle-book dated 1703; the design itself being worked in tent-stitch.

Among other stitches used for grounds are the long flat satin-stitch familiar in Japanese embroideries of all periods, and laid-stitches, *i.e.*, those formed of long threads "laid" on the satin or silk foundation, and held down by short "couching" stitches placed at intervals. Laid-stitch grounds, however, are oftener seen in foreign embroideries, especially Italian and Spanish, than in English examples.

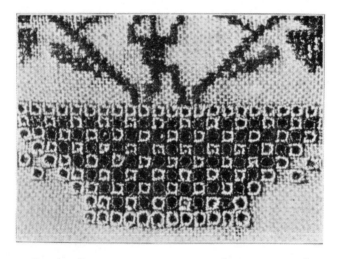

Fig. 63.—Eyelet-hole-stitch: from a Sampler dated 1811.

Although tapestry embroidery backgrounds are in most cases worked "solid," that is, entirely covered with close-set stitches forming an even surface, they are occasionally found to be filled in with some variety of open-stitch, as exemplified by Plate XV. Sometimes the lace-like effect is produced by covering the foundation material with a surface stitch; the first row being a buttonhole-stitch, worked into the stuff so as to form the basis of the succeeding rows of simple lace or knotting stitches. The last row is again worked into the foundation. When, however, a linen canvas of

FIG. 64.—TAPESTRY EMBROIDERY (UPPER PORTION). ABOUT 1640.

Formerly in the Author's possession.

rather open mesh was the material of the picture or panel, it was not unusual to whip or buttonhole over the threads with fine silk, a process resulting in a honeycomb-like series of small eyelet holes, as shown in the enlargement, Fig. 63. This is taken from an early nineteenth-century sampler, but the stitch is precisely similar to that seen in embroideries of the seventeenth and eighteenth centuries.

Figures in Raised Needlework

The high relief portions of the embroidery known as "stump" or "stamp" work, which is popularly supposed to have been invented by the nuns of Little Gidding, appear to have been almost invariably worked separately on stout linen stretched in a frame, and applied when completed. The design was sketched, or transferred, by means of something equivalent to our carbonised paper, on the linen, padded with hair or wool kept in position by a lattice-work of crossing threads, and the raised foundation, or "stump," thus formed covered with close lace-stitches, or with satin or silk, which, in its turn, was partly or entirely covered with embroidery, generally in long-and-short stitch. When the figures were finished a paper was pasted at the back to obviate any risk of frayed or loosened stitches, and they were cut out and fastened into their proper places in the design which had been drawn on or transferred to the silk, satin, or canvas foundation of the actual picture. The lines of attachment are adroitly concealed by couchings of fine cord or gimp.

In some pieces of stump embroidery the heads and hands of the figures are of carved wood covered in most instances with a close network of lace-stitch, or with satin or silk, on which the eyes and mouth are either painted or embroidered. In the more elaborate specimens, however, the satin is merely a foundation for embroidery in long-and-short or split-stitch, the latter being a variety of the ordinary stem-stitch, in which the needle is brought out through, instead of at the side of, the preceding stitch. The features of faces worked in either of these stitches are generally indicated by carefully

Fig. 65.—Face worked in Split-stitch : Enlarged from Embroidery
reproduced in Fig. 64.

directed lines of stem or chain-stitching worked over the ground-stitch. This latter when well worked forms a surface scarcely distinguishable from satin in its smoothness. The Figs. 65 and 66, which are enlargements of portions of the embroidery illustrated in Fig. 64, show examples of this mode of working faces.

Knot-Stitches

Knot-stitches—these, by the way, have no connection with the knotting-work popular at the end of the seventeenth century—are introduced freely into the stump-work pictures to represent the hair of the human figures, together with the woolly coats of sheep and the sundry and divers unclassified animals invariably found in this

FIG. 66.—FACE WORKED IN SPLIT-STITCH: ENLARGED FROM LOWER PORTION (NOT REPRODUCED) OF FIG. 64.

type of embroidered picture.   These knots or knotted stitches range from the small, tightly-worked French knots which, when closely massed, produce a sufficiently realistic imitation of a fleece, to the long bullion knots formed by twisting the silk thread ten or twelve times round the needle before drawing the latter through the loops. The sheep (enlarged from Fig. 64) in Fig. 67 shows very clearly the effect of the massed French knots.   The longer knot-stitches are found to be arranged in even loops sewn closely together, or are worked loosely and placed irregularly to meet the requirements of the design. Knot-stitches of all kinds are seen, too, in the foliage, grass, and mossy banks, although for these couchings of loops of fine cord, untwisted silk and gimp, as well as of purl, seem to have been equally popular. At a later period, that is, towards the middle of the eighteenth century, chenille replaced knot-stitches, couched loops, and purl for the purpose, but it proved much less satisfactory both as regards appearance and durability.

FIG. 67.—KNOTTED-STITCH : ENLARGED FROM EMBROIDERY
REPRODUCED IN FIG. 64.

Looped-stitches are also used to indicate flowing ringlets, for which the bullion knots would be too formal, as may be seen in Figs. 65 and 66. The loops in these examples are of partly untwisted gimp. In flat embroidery, it may be mentioned, the hair is frequently worked in long-and-short or split-stitch, or in short, flat satin-stitches, the lines whereof are cleverly arranged to follow the twists of the curls. In this way the hair of the lady, shown on an enlarged scale in Fig. 66, is worked.

Plush-Stitch

This is a modern name for the stitch used in the Stuart period embroideries for fur robes and the coats of certain beasts. It is also known as velvet, rug, and raised stitch. To carry it out a series of loops is worked over a small mesh or a knitting pin, each loop being secured to the foundation stuff by a tent or cross-stitch, and when the necessary number of rows is completed, the loops are cut as in the raised Berlin wool-work of early Victorian days. In this stitch the ermine of the king's robe in Plate XVIII. is worked, the black stitches meant to represent the little tails having been put in after the completion of the white silk ground.

Embroidery in Purl and Metallic Threads

Purl, both that of uncovered metal and that variety wherein the corkscrew-like tube is cased with silk, was generally cut into pieces of the desired length, which were threaded on the needle and sewn down either flat or in loops, according to the design. The greater part of the beautiful piece of embroidery illustrated in Plate XXIII. is carried out in coloured purl, applied in pieces sufficiently long to follow the curves of the pattern. A small example of looped purl-work is shown in the left-hand upper corner of Fig. 66.

Purl embroidery, when at all on an elaborate scale, was worked in a frame and "applied," although the slighter portions of a design were often executed on the picture itself. The system of working all the heavier parts of such embroideries separately and adding them piece by piece, as it were, until the whole was complete, accounts, of course, for the extreme rarity of a "drawn" or puckered ground in old needlework pictures and panels.

Besides purl, gold and silver "passing" often appears in certain sections of the work. "Passing" is wire sufficiently thin and flexible to be passed through instead of couched down on the foundation material, and with it such devices as rayed suns and moons are often embroidered in long-and-short stitch. A thicker kind of metallic thread was employed for couching, this being made in the same manner as the Japanese thread so largely used in modern work, save that a thin ribbon of real gold took the place of the strip of gilt paper as a casing for the silk thread.

Water is sometimes represented by lengths of silver purl stretched tightly across a flat surface of satin or laid-stitches, but not infrequently, instead of the purl, sheets of talc are laid over the silken stitchery. The water in Susannah's bath (Plate XIV.) is covered with talc, hence it appears light coloured in the reproduction.

When a metallic lustre was needed, the plumules of peacocks' feathers were occasionally employed, especially in the bodies of butterflies and caterpillars, but these unfortunately have almost invariably suffered from the depredations of a small insect, and it is seldom that more remains of them in old embroideries than a few dilapidated and minute fragments, often barely recognisable for what they are.

Lace-Stitches

The needle-point lace-stitches, so profusely used in the dresses and decorative accessories of the figures in Stuart embroideries, are, as a rule, of a close and rather heavy type. Sometimes they are found to be worked directly on the picture or panel as surface stitches, in the manner already described as adopted for backgrounds; but it was undoubtedly more usual to work the ruffles,

Fig. 68.—Embroidery Picture. A Squire and his Lady. Signed M. C. Dated 1657.

Mr Minet.

This embroidery, which bears the initials "M. C." and the date 1657 in pearls, is notable for the variety of stitches which find a place upon it. The central figures are dressed in elaborate costumes, the lady's robe of yellow satin being embroidered with coloured flowers and decked with pearls, laces, and flowers, an attire altogether inconsistent with the Puritanical times in which she lived.

sleeves, flower-petals, butterfly-wings, etc., separately, fastening them into their proper places when finished. Stiffenings of fine wire were generally sewn round the extreme edge of any part intended to stand away from the background. A most interesting variety of

FIG. 69.—HAIR OF UNRAVELLED SILK: ENLARGEMENT OF PORTION OF EMBROIDERY REPRODUCED IN FIG. 64.

lace-stitches may be seen in the costume of the boy shown in the enlargement (Fig. 69), taken from the panel reproduced in Fig. 64. The small illustration (Fig. 61) heading this chapter illustrates quite a different kind of lace-stitch, to wit, the hollie-point, which, originally confined to church embroidery, was during the seventeenth century used to ornament under-garments and babies' christening-robes.

Bead Embroidery

The actual stitchery in the old embroideries that are worked entirely, or almost entirely, in beads, is of an extremely simple description. In the majority of pieces the work is applied as in the case of the stump embroideries, the beads being threaded and sewn down on the framed linen, either flatly or over padding. In the less elaborate class of embroideries, however, the beads are sewn directly on the satin ground; but when this plan has been adopted the design is rarely padded at all, although small portions of it, such as cravats, girdle-tassels, and garter-knots, are found to be detached from the rest of the work. This is for the most part executed with long strings of threaded beads couched down in close-set rows. Plate XXI. represents an excellent specimen of flat and raised bead-work combined with purl embroidery. See also Fig. 53.

Groundwork Tracings

The first stage of an embroidered picture is well illustrated in Fig. 70, which is worthy of careful study. The original is a piece of satin measuring $9\frac{1}{2} \times 8$ in., and on this the design has been traced by a pointed stylus, the deep incised lines made in the thick material having been coloured black, probably by a transferring medium similar to carbonised paper. The shadows have been added with a brush, evidently wielded by an experienced hand, for not only are they gradated in the original, but there are no signs of any difficulty in dealing with the flow of colour on the absorbent

textile.   The   subject   of   the   picture   is   said   to   be   the   Princess
Mary   and   the   Prince   William   of   Orange.

Implements Used

It   is   probable   that   some   details   in   the   picture—acorns,   fruit,

FIG. 70.—GROUNDWORK TRACING FOR EMBROIDERED PICTURE.   17TH CENTURY.
Mr E. Hennell.

and   the   like—were   worked   with   the   aid   of   the   curious   little
implements   shown   in   Fig.   71.   These   are   thimble-shaped   moulds
of   thin,   hard   wood,   which   have   two   rows   of   holes   pierced   round
their   base.   Through   these   holes   are   passed   the   threads   which
form   the   foundation   of   the   rows   of   lace   or   knotting-stitches   that

are worked with the needle round and round the mould until it is completely covered. The knotted purses of the seventeenth and eighteenth centuries were possibly made on moulds of this kind.

FIG. 71.—MOULDS FOR KNOTTED OR LACE WORK, WITH SILK SPOOLS AND CASE.

The plate shows two of these queer little objects, as well as a long spool or bobbin with ancient silks of various colours still wound on it, the spool-case belonging to it, and two pieces of knotted-work in different stages of development.

II.—The Stitchery of Samplers, with a Note on their Materials

"Sad sewers make sad samplers. We'll be sorry
Down to our fingers'-ends and 'broider emblems
Native to desolation—cypress sprays,
Yew-tufts and hectic leaves of various autumn
And bitter tawny rue, and bent blackthorns."

The Soldier of Fortune.—LORD DE TABLEY.

Cut and Drawn-Work

THE open-work stitchery, which is so important and pleasing a feature of the seventeenth-century sampler, is of two kinds; that is, *double* cut-work—the Italian *punto tagliato*—in which both warp and woof threads are removed, save for a few necessary connecting bars, and *single* cut-work—*punto tirato*—wherein but one set of threads is withdrawn. The first type (which is probably the "rare Italian cut-work" mentioned in "The Needle's Excellency") is the immediate ancestor of needle-point lace, and is the kind that is oftenest met with in the oldest and finest samplers; the second approaches more nearly to the drawn-thread embroidery worked both abroad and at home at the present day.

In executing real double cut-work, after the surplus material has been cut away, the supporting or connecting threads are over-

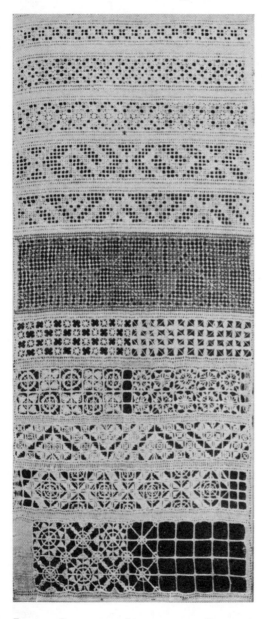

FIG. 72.—DRAWN-WORK SAMPLER. 17TH CENTURY,

cast, the edges of the cut linen buttonholed, and the spaces within this framework filled in with lace-stitches, simple or elaborate. In the best specimens of samplers the effect is sometimes enhanced by portions of the pattern being detached from the ground, as in the upper part of the beautiful sampler illustrated in Fig. 72.[1] These loose pieces usually have as basis a row of buttonhole-stitches worked into the linen, but in some examples the lace has been worked quite separately and sewn on. The mode of working both double and single cutwork is shown plainly in the two enlargements (Figs. 73 and 74), which are of parts of samplers probably worked about 1660.

[1] A very good example of a sampler in drawn-work, in which the floral form of decoration is entirely absent, save in the sixth row (the pinks), which is in green silk, the rest being in white. That the sampler was intended as a pattern is evident from some of the rows being unfinished.

There is a third and much simpler type of open-work occasionally found on seventeenth-century samplers, which is carried out by piercing the linen with a stiletto and overcasting the resulting holes so as to produce a series of bird's-eye or eyelet stitches. All three varieties of open-stitch are frequently seen in combination with that short, flat satin-stitch, which, when worked in a diaper pattern with white thread or silk on a white ground, is sometimes called damask-stitch. This pretty combination of stitches appears in Plate VI., and also in the enlargement (Fig. 74) already referred to.

FIG. 73.—CUT AND DRAWN-WORK: ENLARGEMENT FROM 17TH-CENTURY SAMPLER.

Back-Stitch

This stitch was largely used in the seventeenth and early eighteenth centuries for the adornment of articles of personal clothing, as well as of quilts and hangings, hence it is natural that it is prominent in the samplers of the period. In the older specimens the bands of back-stitch patterns are worked with exquisite neatness, both sides being precisely alike; but in those of later date signs of carelessness are apparent, and the reverse side is somewhat untidy. In no sampler examined by the writer, however, has the back-stitch been produced by working a chain-stitch on the wrong side of the linen, as is the case in some of the embroidered garments of the period.

The samplers illustrated in Plates III. and VII. are noticeable

for their good bands of back-stitching.   A small section of Fig. 6
is shown on an enlarged scale in Fig. 75.   In some modern text-
books of embroidery, it may be added, the old reversible or two-
sided back-stitch is distinguished as Holbein-stitch.

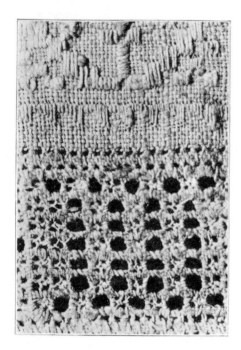

FIG. 74.—SATIN-STITCH AND COMBINATION OF
   TYPES OF OPEN-WORK: ENLARGED FROM
   THE SAMPLER REPRODUCED IN FIG.
   17TH CENTURY.

Alphabet-Stitches

The stitches used for the
lettering on samplers are three
in number, to wit, cross-stitch,
bird's-eye-stitch and satin-stitch.
Of the first there are two
varieties, the ordinary cross-
stitch, known in later years as
sampler-stitch, and the much
neater kind, in which the crossed
stitches form a perfect little
square on the wrong side.   This
daintiest of marking stitches is
rarely seen on samplers later than
the eighteenth century.

The satin-stitch alphabets
are worked in short flat stitches,
not over padding, according to
the modern method of initial
embroidering, and the letters are generally square rather than curved
in outline.   The bird's-eye-stitch, when used for alphabets, varies
greatly in degree of fineness.   In some instances the holes are
very closely overcast with short, even stitches, but in others the
latter are alternately long and short, so that each "eyelet" or
"bird's-eye" is the centre, as it were, of a star of ray-like stitches.

Darning-Stitches

The stitches exemplifying the mode of darning damask, cambric, or linen had usually a sampler entirely devoted to them, and at one period—the end of the eighteenth century—it seems to have been a fairly general custom that a girl should work one as a companion to the ordinary sampler of lettering and patterns. The specimen darns

FIG. 75.—BACK-STITCH : ENLARGEMENT OF PORTION OF SAMPLER IN FIG. 6. 17TH CENTURY. TWICE ACTUAL SIZE.

on such a sampler are, as a rule, arranged in squares or crosses round some centre device, a bouquet or basket of flowers for instance, or it may be merely the initials of the worker in a shield. The two samplers (Fig. 76 and Plate XXIV.) are typical examples of their kind, although perhaps the ornamental parts of the designs are a little more fanciful than in the majority of those met with.

The best worked—not necessarily the most elaborately embellished —of this particular class of sampler has small pieces of the material actually cut out and the holes filled up with darning, but in inferior

ones the stuff is left untouched, and the darn is simply worked on
the linen, tammy cloth, or tiffany itself.   This is a very much easier
method and the appearance is better; but the darns so made are,
after all, but imitations of the real thing.   For the damask darns
fine silk of two colours is invariably used, and in the properly
worked examples both sides are alike, save, of course, for the reversal
of the damask effect, as in woven damask.

The centre designs in the two samplers illustrated are worked
in fine darning-stitches of divers kinds, outlined with chain and stem
stitches.   Here and there a few other stitches are introduced, as in
the stem of the rose in Fig. 76, where French knots are used to
produce the mossy appearance.   The centre basket in this sampler
is worked in lines of chain-stitching crossing each other lattice
fashion.   Both the samplers have the initials of their workers, and in
that shown in Fig. 76 the date (1802) also, neatly darned into one
of the crosses formed by the damask patterns.

Darning-samplers are usually square, or nearly square, in shape,
and are simply finished with a single line of hem-stitching at the
edge, but some of the older ones are ornamented with a broader
band of drawn-work as border; while a few have examples of
drawn-work, alternating with squares and crosses of darning, in the
body of the sampler.   A small section of such a sampler, dated 1785,
is illustrated on an enlarged scale in Fig. 77.   It has a series of
small conventional leaf patterns worked in single drawn-work, and
edged with a scalloping worked in chain-stitch with green silk.   The
ground of this particular sampler is thin linen, but the muslin-like stuff
known as tiffany is that used for the foundation of nine darning-samplers
out of ten.

Tent and Cross-Stitches

Neither tent-stitch nor tapestry-stitch appears to have been
largely introduced in sampler-embroidery at any period; still, portions

FIG. 76.—DARNING SAMPLER. SIGNED M. M., T. B., J. F. DATED 1802.

The late Mrs Head.

of a few specimens worked during the early and middle years of the eighteenth century are executed in one or other of these stitches. Tent-stitch, for instance, plays an important part in the wreath border of Fig. 9. The beautifully shaded leaves are all worked in this way, as are many of the flowers, other varieties of grounding or cushion-stitches being used for the rest of the border. The Commandments, which the wreath enframes, are worked in cross-stitch. This last-named stitch in its earliest form is worked over a single thread, and produces a close and solid effect when closely massed, or, as may be seen in many sampler maps, very fine lines when worked in single rows. Ordinary cross-stitch taken over two threads is, of course, the familiar stitch in which nineteenth-century samplers are entirely worked, whence arises its second name of sampler-stitch.

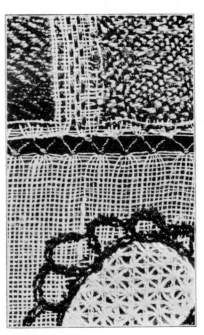

FIG. 77.—ENLARGED PORTION OF A DARNING SAMPLER. DATED 1785.

A pretty and—in sampler embroidery — uncommon stitch is that in which the crowned lions in the samplers of Mary and Lydia Johnson (Figs. 35 and 36) are worked. This stitch is formed of two cross-stitches superimposed diagonally, and since its revival in the Berlin wool era has been known by the names of star-stitch and leviathan-stitch.

Various Stitches

Besides the stitches already enumerated and described, sundry and divers others are found on samplers of various periods. Satin-stitch, for instance, is used for borders and other parts of designs, as well as for alphabets. Long-and-short - stitch, frequently very irregularly executed, seems to have been popular for the embroidery of the wreaths and garlands that make gay many of the later eighteenth - century samplers. Stem-stitch, save for such minor details as flower-stalks and tendrils, is not often seen ; but the wreath-borders of a limited number of eighteenth-century samplers are done entirely in this stitch, worked in lines round and round, or up and down, each leaf and petal until the whole is filled in. Stem-stitch, it should be explained, is, to all intents and purposes, the same as "outline" or "crewel" stitch. The latter name, however, is likewise applied to long-and-short or plumage stitch by some writers on embroidery.

Laid-stitches may also be included in the list of stitches occurring occasionally in samplers, although it is rarely met with in its more elaborate forms. A sampler dated 1808 has two baskets (of flowers) worked in long laid-stitches of brown silk couched with yellow silk, the effect of wicker-work being produced with some success by this plan, and similar unambitious examples appear in some samplers of rather earlier date.

The portion of a sampler shown in Fig. 2 is interesting by reason of the fact that it is worked in knots, a form of stitchery comparatively rare, save in those unclassifiable pieces of embroidery which are neither pictures nor samplers, but possess some of the features of both.

Materials

Linen, bleached or unbleached, but, of course, always hand-woven, is the foundation material of the early samplers. It varies greatly in texture, from a coarse, canvas-like kind to a fine and closely woven sort of about the same stoutness as good modern pillow-case linen. The stitchery of these oldest samplers is executed in linen thread or a somewhat loosely twisted silk, often scarcely coarser than our nineteenth-century " machine silk," although, on the other hand, a very thick and irregularly spun type is occasionally seen.

About 1725 linen of a peculiar yellow colour and rather harsh texture came into vogue ; but this went out of fashion in a few years, and towards the end of the eighteenth century the strong and durable linen was almost entirely superseded by an ugly and moth-attracting stuff called indifferently tammy, tammy cloth, bolting cloth, and, when woven in a specially narrow width, sampler canvas. The stitchery on samplers of this date is almost invariably executed with silk, although in a few of the coarser ones fine untwisted crewel is substituted. Tiffany, the thin, muslin-like material mentioned in connection with darning-samplers, was at this period used also for small delicately wrought samplers of the ordinary type.

Early in the nineteenth century very coarsely woven linen and linen canvas came into fashion again, and for some time were nearly as popular as the woollen tammy ; while, about 1820, twisted crewels of the crudest dyes replaced in a great measure the soft toned silks. Next followed the introduction of cotton canvas and Berlin wool, and with them vanished the last remaining vestige of the exquisite stitchery and well-balanced designs of earlier generations, and the sampler, save in a most degraded form, ceased to exist.

Index

A CATALOGUE OF SELECTED DOVER BOOKS
IN ALL FIELDS OF INTEREST

A CATALOGUE OF SELECTED DOVER
BOOKS IN ALL FIELDS OF INTEREST

RACKHAM'S COLOR ILLUSTRATIONS FOR WAGNER'S RING. Rackham's finest mature work—all 64 full-color watercolors in a faithful and lush interpretation of the *Ring*. Full-sized plates on coated stock of the paintings used by opera companies for authentic staging of Wagner. Captions aid in following complete Ring cycle. Introduction. 64 illustrations plus vignettes. 72pp. 8⅝ x 11¼. 23779-6 Pa. $6.00

CONTEMPORARY POLISH POSTERS IN FULL COLOR, edited by Joseph Czestochowski. 46 full-color examples of brilliant school of Polish graphic design, selected from world's first museum (near Warsaw) dedicated to poster art. Posters on circuses, films, plays, concerts all show cosmopolitan influences, free imagination. Introduction. 48pp. 9⅜ x 12¼. 23780-X Pa. $6.00

GRAPHIC WORKS OF EDVARD MUNCH, Edvard Munch. 90 haunting, evocative prints by first major Expressionist artist and one of the greatest graphic artists of his time: *The Scream, Anxiety, Death Chamber, The Kiss, Madonna,* etc. Introduction by Alfred Werner. 90pp. 9 x 12. 23765-6 Pa. $5.00

THE GOLDEN AGE OF THE POSTER, Hayward and Blanche Cirker. 70 extraordinary posters in full colors, from Maitres de l'Affiche, Mucha, Lautrec, Bradley, Cheret, Beardsley, many others. Total of 78pp. 9⅜ x 12¼. 22753-7 Pa. $5.95

THE NOTEBOOKS OF LEONARDO DA VINCI, edited by J. P. Richter. Extracts from manuscripts reveal great genius; on painting, sculpture, anatomy, sciences, geography, etc. Both Italian and English. 186 ms. pages reproduced, plus 500 additional drawings, including studies for *Last Supper,* Sforza monument, etc. 860pp. 7⅞ x 10¾. (Available in U.S. only) 22572-0, 22573-9 Pa., Two-vol. set $15.90

THE CODEX NUTTALL, as first edited by Zelia Nuttall. Only inexpensive edition, in full color, of a pre-Columbian Mexican (Mixtec) book. 88 color plates show kings, gods, heroes, temples, sacrifices. New explanatory, historical introduction by Arthur G. Miller. 96pp. 11⅜ x 8½. (Available in U.S. only) 23168-2 Pa. $7.50

UNE SEMAINE DE BONTÉ, A SURREALISTIC NOVEL IN COLLAGE, Max Ernst. Masterpiece created out of 19th-century periodical illustrations, explores worlds of terror and surprise. Some consider this Ernst's greatest work. 208pp. 8⅛ x 11. 23252-2 Pa. $5.00

THE STANDARD BOOK OF QUILT MAKING AND COLLECTING, Marguerite Ickis. Full information, full-sized patterns for making 46 traditional quilts, also 150 other patterns. Quilted cloths, lame, satin quilts, etc. 483 illustrations. 273pp. 6⅞ x 9⅝. 20582-7 Pa. $3.95

ENCYCLOPEDIA OF VICTORIAN NEEDLEWORK, S. Caulfield, Blanche Saward. Simply inexhaustible gigantic alphabetical coverage of every traditional needlecraft—stitches, materials, methods, tools, types of work; definitions, many projects to be made. 1200 illustrations; double-columned text. 697pp. 8⅛ x 11. 22800-2, 22801-0 Pa., Two-vol. set $12.00

MECHANICK EXERCISES ON THE WHOLE ART OF PRINTING, Joseph Moxon. First complete book (1683-4) ever written about typography, a compendium of everything known about printing at the latter part of 17th century. Reprint of 2nd (1962) Oxford Univ. Press edition. 74 illustrations. Total of 550pp. 6⅛ x 9¼. 23617-X Pa. $7.95

PAPERMAKING, Dard Hunter. Definitive book on the subject by the foremost authority in the field. Chapters dealing with every aspect of history of craft in every part of the world. Over 320 illustrations. 2nd, revised and enlarged (1947) edition. 672pp. 5⅜ x 8½. 23619-6 Pa. $7.95

THE ART DECO STYLE, edited by Theodore Menten. Furniture, jewelry, metalwork, ceramics, fabrics, lighting fixtures, interior decors, exteriors, graphics from pure French sources. Best sampling around. Over 400 photographs. 183pp. 8⅜ x 11¼. 22824-X Pa. $5.00

Prices subject to change without notice.

Available at your book dealer or write for free catalogue to Dept. GI, Dover Publications, Inc., 180 Varick St., N.Y., N.Y. 10014. Dover publishes more than 175 books each year on science, elementary and advanced mathematics, biology, music, art, literary history, social sciences and other areas.